COWBOY BITES

A ROUGH RIDERS COOKBOOK

COWBOY BITES

A ROUGH RIDERS COOKBOOK

SHORT STORIES BY
NEW YORK TIMES BESTSELLING AUTHOR

LORELEI JAMES

RECIPES FROM *USA TODAY* BESTSELLING AUTHOR
SUZANNE M. JOHNSON

COWBOY BITES

Lorelei's Foreword

Howdy readers! Are you in for a treat with this cookbook! I'm thrilled that Suzanne Johnson agreed to provide the tantalizing recipes, chock-full of her specialty of down-home dishes that'll satisfy everyone at the dinner table.

How did this project come about, you ask? Well, it started with a little thing called cowboy candy...

For several years, I've been blessed to spend almost a week at the beach with an amazing group of friends. And because we're such clever writers, we christened ourselves the Beach Babes.

In between all the laughter, movie marathons, dance parties, Jell-O shots, drinking, business discussions, shopping excursions, and late night talks, we've been lucky to have Suzanne join us, and feed not only our bodies, but our souls with her delicious cooking.

I'm not the first author to collaborate with Suzanne, and I'll admit to some... jealousy about that, sitting at the counter in the kitchen over the years, hearing Suzanne discussing recipes for her cookbooks with Lexi Blake and J Kenner. It just so happened she was working on Larissa Ione's cookbook that year. Suzanne had created a new condiment and had brought along a sample to share. She asked for an honest opinion on her "candied jalapeños." My brain immediately jumped to what we out here in the West call that: cowboy candy.

After just one bite of such hot/sweet perfection, I casually asked, "Is this for Larissa's cookbook?" Suzanne shrugged and said, "I'm not sure." Then I actually yelled – "NO! It's mine! I want it for MY cookbook." Yes, I yelled at the poor sweet woman—not my proudest moment, people. I think we sort of simultaneously said "cowboy candy" and since yours truly is the western/cowboy writer of our Beach Babes bunch, she understood why I'd laid claim to it. Then Suzanne gifted me with her big smile and said, "You want to do a cookbook with me?"

That's how *Cowboy Bites* was born.

Since Suzanne had other cookbooks in the oven—*hahaha*—with Kristen Proby and Kristen Ashley, I had to wait my turn (hard keeping it a secret!). But we had pretty much nailed down exactly the type of cookbook we wanted it to be: homestyle cooking you'd find at the McKay family's table.

Food has always been a part of my stories, so the difficulty for me was choosing which couples to revisit because I wanted to do them all! However, for this project, I didn't set out to write one continuous story, but more "slice of life" pieces where we pop in and see what our beloved McKay couples are up to after their happily-ever-after.

So *Cupcake Up* takes place within the first year that Cord and AJ are married. *Grilled Hard* is set when Carter and Macie are expecting their third child. Colby and Channing's story, *Long Hard Boil,* is set around Channing's 40th birthday. *All Jammed Up* features Keely and Jack and all four of their little hellions. Likewise for Colt and Indy in *Recipe for Trouble,* and their three kiddos. *Unbreak My Dishes* is set directly after the end of Boone and Sierra's book. I had so much fun using a play on words for each one of their titles from the Rough Riders series.

My biggest gratitude goes to the wonderful Suzanne Johnson, who has been an enthusiastic partner about this project from the get-go. Although, it KILLED me when she texted me pictures of the dishes she created for this cookbook because I just wanted to devour them.

I want to thank my fantastic Team LJ – Lindsey Faber, for editing the stories, Meredith Blair, for another amazing cover and interior pages, and Kim O'Connor, PA extraordinaire, for doing everything else so I can write.

Huge thanks also to Evil Eye/Blue Box Press—Liz Berry, Jillian Stein, M.J. Rose, Kim Guidroz, Nancy MacDonald, Jessie Marony, Asha Hossain, and Jenn Watson of Social Butterfly.

And thanks to my readers, who have kept the McKay family in their hearts for years...I hope you enjoy another Rough Riders installment!

XOXO

L~

Table of Contents

CHAPTER 1

CUPCAKE UP

AJ McKay shifted in her seat as Karen Souther, president of the SPAT—Sundance Parents Assisting Teachers—chirped about members' responsibilities and recounted the group's mission statement and bylaws.

She couldn't help but wonder how much the rehashing of the rules was solely for her benefit, since she was the newest member to their club, not to mention the youngest.

Joining SPAT hadn't even crossed her mind until an excited Kyler had brought the membership form home to *his mom* the second day of first grade.

Like she could've said no after that.

She'd gotten used to Ky calling her Mom after she'd married his dad last year. But this was her first public foray as Kyler's parent—god knew writing a check was her husband Cord's idea of group participation.

Maybe he had the right idea.

AJ wasn't much of a "joiner," mostly due to her shyness. Yet it seemed strange that despite spending most of her life in Crook County, she felt like an outsider in this group. She'd seen a few of these women around town, but none were friendly with other members of the McKay family, nor had any of them sought out her services as a masseuse.

They could use one of your massages, baby doll. They're an uptight bunch.

She told her husband's smarmy voice inside her head to shut up.

"Thank you, Mary, for the treasurer's report. Onto old business. The K through fifth grade Autumn Festival is at the end of the week. As in years past, each classroom will have a themed booth, which functions as a home base for the students. What SPAT sponsors is an entirely separate aspect for the festival. With that in mind, let's go over the final details for the committee assignments."

Final list? How could it be a final list when this was SPAT's first meeting? AJ started to have a bad feeling she'd missed something.

"Mary and Rhetta"—Karen pointed to the blonde who'd recited the treasurer's report and the brunette sitting next to her at the front table—"are in charge of decorating. Anything noteworthy to report?"

"The party store in Spearfish offered us a substantial discount for all the paper goods and decorations," the dark-haired one replied. She giggled. "I think the manager has a crush on you, Karen. He asked if you were still single."

A chorus of oohs rang out.

Karen rolled her eyes. "Like being the wife of a retail store manager holds any appeal for me. I'd rather stay divorced."

AJ sent a furtive glance to the other women in attendance, but no one else seemed bothered by the snotty and mean comment.

"Nevertheless, I'm grateful for the discount," Karen said breezily. They discussed the placement of streamers, balloons and banners for what seemed like an eternity. Finally Karen glanced at her notes and then back up. "Desi. What's the status on the craft booth?"

A Native American woman threw her long, black braid over her shoulder and turned to address the group, instead of Karen. "The students can choose from creating a face on a pumpkin-shaped gourd or twisting a scarecrow doll out of straw. My contact donated the materials for both crafts."

"The committee had decided on *three* crafts for the children to choose from and you are telling me there's only two?" Karen said sharply.

Desi slowly faced Karen. "I'm telling you, President Souther, to be grateful for two 'quick, autumn themed' crafts I procured that SPAT doesn't have to pay for," she said coolly. "Besides, we don't have enough volunteers to run a third booth anyway."

Silence.

Instead of saying thank you, Karen studied her notes. Then she addressed the two blonde women in the front row to her left. "You're up, Tayla and Chrissy. Tell me about the carnival-style games."

"For grades three through five, we opted for a target golf game and a ring toss. For kindergarten through second grade, there will be the fish cup game and a lollipop tree. Barring snow, it'll be best to host the games outside."

"And prizes for those games?"

"We purchased gift cards from Dairy Queen."

AJ frowned. Gift cards? Nothing a six-year-old liked better than receiving a gift they had to ask an adult for help to use.

Karen practically clapped. "Excellent! Moving on—"

"Wait."

Every head in the room swiveled to look at AJ. She felt the blush rise up her neck, but she kept her chin level and her voice strong.

"Questions are left for the end," Tayla said snottily. "If you bothered to follow procedure—"

"It's all right, Tayla," Karen inserted. "Go ahead...I'm sorry, I've forgotten your name."

"AJ McKay. I have two questions, actually. First, how many gift cards and what's the monetary amount on each card?"

"Four gift cards, each worth twenty-five dollars," Chrissy retorted. "Is that all right with you?"

AJ felt the sting from that strike all the way where she sat in the back row. Still, she smiled. "That depends on how the winners are chosen?"

"Like they always have been; they're the highest scoring winners of the carnival games."

That didn't clear up a damn thing. "So out of two hundred students, only four can win prizes? There isn't a general participation prize for each student?"

"Oh for godsake, did you *read* any of the emails?" Mary from the front table demanded. "We've been discussing this for weeks."

Tempting to let this nest of vipers drag her into the bottom of the pit so she could bite back. But that's probably what they expected, so she refused to give them the satisfaction. "Really? That is news to me. Apparently I've been excluded from the email loop, which I'm sure was just a technical oversight, since none of you can remember my name."

"Or it's an oversight on *your* part because you didn't think to check your spam folder," Mary said. "I don't see why you think you can just show up and offer your opinions when all the subcommittees have already done the work."

"This ain't our first rodeo, cowgirl," Tayla added.

Several women snickered.

"If you'll allow us to get through the committee assignment reports," Karen said, "then I'd be happy to answer any of your questions at the end."

AJ had no choice except to agree.

Karen pointed to a pair of brunettes sitting in front of Desi. "Melanie and Trista...any issues with the cider stand?"

"No. Everything is good to go. We've rounded up enough punch bowls for the cold drinks and each one will have dry ice. We've also tracked down enough coffee urns for the hot cider."

"Great. Nina and Junie? Where are we on donations for the cake walk?"

Nina and Junie looked at each other. Then Nina, a robust redhead spoke. "Well, as you know, each classroom is having their own party, and that requires multiple contributions from every family, so we are a little...short on donations."

"How short?"

"We've confirmed ten."

"That's half of what I assigned you."

Junie, Nina's frumpy seatmate, held up her hands. "We know. We're working on it."

Karen's gaze narrowed. "If you can't acquire the agreed-upon amount of donations, then it's your responsibility to bridge the quota gap yourselves. For the committee's sake, I need assurance that we won't have any disappointed students."

Nina nodded, a bit glumly.

AJ leaned forward and tapped Junie on the shoulder. "I can donate however many cakes you're short and—"

"While the offer is appreciated, AJ...you're *not* a designated member of that subcommittee," Karen interjected, "and they have the experience to handle it themselves." *Unlike you* went unsaid.

"I don't appear to be a member of any subcommittee, so why don't you just assign me to that one since they need help?"

"If you were paying attention during the recitation of our bylaws, you'd realize that's not how we do things. Committee assignments were handed down last month by the elected officers. However, we'll keep you in mind for the next SPAT event."

"There's nothing that needs to be done now? No room for my help on any of the subcommittees?"

Nina started to face her, but snapped back around when Karen pointedly cleared her throat.

"Since you're so...insistent on participation, I imagine the decorating committee could find something useful for you to contribute, couldn't you, Mary?"

"Sure," Mary said. "We could use a few extra haybales for atmosphere. I'm sure they're in abundant supply on the massive McKay ranch."

"Haybales? That's it?"

"Unless you want to offer free massages to committee members? Since word is that you own a massage parlor," Rhetta added.

A massage parlor? Wow. Okay. So that's how it was gonna be. She mentally dropped her gloves and shifted into a fighting stance. Then she smiled—all teeth. "Providing haybales would be great. Thank you for the opportunity to contribute."

And she fumed for the remainder of the discussions.

No surprise she didn't stick around to chitchat after the meeting ended.

Cord McKay heard AJ slamming dishes when he walked into the house. He leaned against the doorjamb between the kitchen and entryway, keeping his distance when he eyed the cooking utensils within her reach. When she paused in her mutterings about haybales, he drawled, "Bad day, darlin'?"

As anticipated, she whirled around brandishing a rolling pin.

Also as anticipated, his body reacted to the sight of his beautiful, sexy wife standing barefoot in their kitchen cooking supper, her white-blonde hair twisted in a messy bun and heat from the stove staining her cheeks. His heart went soft even as his dick went hard.

For the millionth time he wondered how he'd gotten so goddamned lucky that all her fire and sweetness was his.

"It was a perfectly fine day up until that SPAT meeting."

Do not say I told you so, man, don't do it.

AJ's icy blue eyes locked onto his when he wisely kept his mouth shut. "I need to rant."

"Rant all you want, baby doll, but first c'mere and gimme a kiss."

"Something wrong with your legs, cowboy, that you can't come here?"

"Besides you're pissed off and holdin' a weapon? There's the other issue that I'm still wearin' my boots and last I knew, you had rules about no shitkickers mucking up your kitchen floor."

She gave him an evil smile. "He can be taught."

Cord raised an eyebrow.

"Oh, don't give me that look. I don't have time for kissing anyway; I gotta get this pie in the oven. Go clean yourself up and let me work off a little more of this mad."

He stepped back into the entryway and sat on the bench to remove his boots.

Kyler crept over to him, holding his finger to his lips.

His son leaned against him and whispered, "She's been workin' off that mad since after school, Dad."

Cord bit back a laugh and wrapped his arm around Ky's waist for a quick hug. He whispered back, "Maybe it'll sweeten her up if you set the table."

"Okay." Kyler straightened and strode into the kitchen. "Heya, Mom. Need help?"

Cord took the steps up to their bedroom two at a time. After stripping out of his work clothes, he showered. Then he shaved, combed his hair, and slipped on a pair of old sweatpants and a plain black T-shirt.

Back downstairs, he found AJ at the sink. Moving in behind her, he curled his hands around the curve of her hips, letting his mouth drift across the warm, sweet-smelling skin of her neck to the slope of her shoulder. "All clean and here to collect my kisses."

"Cord...wait—" ended on a breathy moan as he sank his teeth into the spot that literally caused her knees to buckle.

He growled, "Done waitin'," and spun her to face him.

AJ twined her arms around his neck and rubbed her cheek against his. "Mmm. Smooth. I love that you shave at night." Pressing kisses up his jawline, she murmured, "Lord, you smell good." Then she slid her fingers into his damp hair and whispered, "My lips are all yours."

Cord could've devoured her. It's likely what she expected. Instead, he kissed her softly. Slowly. Sweetly. Losing himself in the way she gave her all to him, regardless if fire raged between them or he gifted her with tenderness. His hands tightened on her hips and she arched into him, all her soft bits perfectly aligned with his hard parts. Since he never knew when Ky would burst in, he forced his hands not to roam, even when his fingers itched to feel her flesh quivering from his touch.

Loud footsteps stopped suddenly behind him. "Geez. Are you kissin' *again?*" Kyler complained. "We haven't even had supper yet!"

AJ ended the kiss with a soft nibble on Cord's bottom lip and mouthed, "Later." Then she said, "I doubt me'n your dad smooching in the kitchen will ruin your appetite, Ky."

"It will if I think about the two of you swappin' spit. Gross."

Cord turned around, smiling at his always-entertaining son. "Where'd you hear that term?"

"Some fifth-grade boys were talkin' about it on the playground." He shook his head. "I don't get it."

"I know you don't, but there'll come a day when you will." He clapped Ky on the shoulder. "Wash up. Supper's ready."

"What're we havin'?"

AJ said, "Philly flank steak rolls."

"And Brussels sprouts?" Ky said hopefully.

She ruffled his hair. "Of course."

The boy tore off toward the bathroom.

His wife chuckled. "Never would've believed that kid's love of Brussels sprouts."

"It's the way you cook 'em, darlin'. I never cared for them before either."

After they ate, Cord helped Ky with his homework. He didn't remember having homework in first grade, but as AJ pointed out, he hadn't been doing third grade math at age six like Kyler was. The kid would need a tutor when he reached algebra; hopefully that'd be later rather than sooner.

During the homework session, AJ paced as she talked on the phone. Cord let her be. It was his night to read a bedtime story and tuck Ky in anyway.

Cord returned downstairs and found AJ putting away the last pan. "Wasn't it my turn to do dishes?

"Yeah. But I was restless." She smiled. "Wanna split a beer?"

"Sure." He popped the top on a bottle of Fat Tire and clasped her hand in his, leading her into the living room. On the couch she curled into him, with her legs across his lap.

She sighed after a healthy swig of beer. "So how was your day?"

"Ranch work, same as any other day. Now tell me what happened at the school that got you all het up."

"It's stupid."

"Tell me anyway."

So she did. After she finished, she swallowed another drink of beer. "I was so infuriated that on the way home, I hatched this plan of dropping off an entire flatbed of haybales. Which I would've turned into the coolest fucking maze the school had ever seen. Then I'd gleefully point out it wasn't SPAT's idea, but mine. But then I realized how much work it'd be, and in the end...I'd just prove the president's point that I can't follow their blasted rules."

"That mean you're just gonna let it go?"

"Hell no." AJ leaned back and her sneaky smile indicated SPAT better look out.

"Good god, woman, what payback are you planning?"

"None. But I did voice my...concerns the about lack of participation prizes to both Ky's teacher, Mrs. Hutchins, and Ginny Jones, the room parent. I offered a solution which they both approved."

"Is this gonna paint a target on your back?"

"With the last name McKay?" She snorted. "There was already a target on my back." She shrugged. "Besides. As Kyler's mom, I'm the first parent of the next generation of McKays to get involved in school activities, but there'll be a whole bunch of them behind me. Just because I'm younger than the SPAT members doesn't mean I'll roll over for them."

Cord captured her chin in his hand, turning her head, forcing her to look at him. "I love you."

AJ blinked at him.

"You make my life better every damn day. Ky's life too."

"Okay. But Cord, honey, why are you telling me what I already know?"

He kissed her, just a teasing brush of his lips. "Because I don't tell you enough." Another sweep of his mouth across hers. "Because I'm a grumpy old man who's a lot better at showin' you how I feel than tellin' you."

"Mmm. I agree that you are very good with this mouth, even when you don't say a single word." Keeping her eyes on his, she slowly licked his bottom lip. "So take me to bed and show me, cowboy."

He hesitated a beat too long.

"What?"

"Can I catch the last of the game? The Broncos are playin' tonight."

She sighed. "The magic is gone...thrown over for Monday Night Football." She drained the beer and stood.

"I'll be up in a bit."

AJ seemed surprised to see him when he walked into their bedroom five minutes later. "How bad were they losing?"

"By two touchdowns."

She flipped the covers back, revealing her nakedness. "Lucky thing I'm ready for you to score."

God. He adored this woman.

He pounced on her.

And scored with her.

Twice.

The next afternoon, after AJ picked Kyler up from school, they stopped at the grocery store to load up on baking supplies.

While AJ debated on using canned frosting versus making her own buttercream frosting, Ky raced off to pick out cereal and frozen waffles.

"AJ?"

She turned and faced the Native woman from yesterday's meeting.

"We didn't get a chance to officially meet after the spat at SPAT yesterday." She offered a wide smile and her hand. "I'm Desi Mears."

"Happy to meet you, Desi. How long have you been volunteering with SPAT?"

"Since my daughter Jocelyn started kindergarten. She's in third grade now."

"Our son Kyler is in first grade."

"You married Cord McKay last year, right?"

AJ cocked her head. "You know that because you're a friend of the McKay family?"

"There's so many of them I could claim to be, and you wouldn't know the difference. But the truth is...it caused a bit of a stir when Sundance Elementary's hottest, unmarried father got hitched to you—a true cowgirl and a local to boot. Broke a lot of hearts." Desi snickered when AJ's eyes widened. "Come on. You *know* your husband's level of attractiveness."

"Yes, I do." She couldn't help but smirk. "I just wasn't aware he had a fan club."

"Oh, trust me, he did. Lots of ogling and sighing when he waited outside to pick up his darling young son from kindergarten. The reason you met with that snotty attitude yesterday at SPAT was because of jealousy. You're younger than all of us and that fine man is all yours." She flashed another smile. "Please don't tell my husband I said that. Anyway, I just wanted to say it is a helpful organization, so don't let one meeting sour your opinion."

"I appreciate your candor, Desi. Yesterday got my hackles up, but I'm regrouping, not quitting."

Desi looked at the twenty pounds of flour, ten pounds of sugar, bottles of food dye, jars of sprinkles, cocoa powder, eggs, butter, carton of whipping cream and packets of shiny cupcake liners in AJ's cart. "Looks like it."

Kyler came down the aisle at full bore, a box of Lucky Charms clutched to his chest and a bag of frozen waffles bouncing against his leg, a girl with long black pigtails chasing him. "Got 'em!" he proudly proclaimed, tossing the box and bag in the cart, then standing guard.

"Mom!" the girl said to Desi. "He took the last box of Lucky Charms."

"You snooze, you lose," Ky shot back.

"Kyler McKay! That is uncalled for."

"Jocelyn, honey, it's just cereal. Go pick something else," Desi said.

"But it's my favorite." Jocelyn turned away, shoulders slumped, and slowly shuffled down the aisle.

AJ waited for her son to do the right thing—without her prompting him.

Sighing, Ky grabbed the box of cereal from the cart and chased after Jocelyn, thrusting it at her before backtracking to the cereal aisle to choose something else.

Desi's gaze met AJ's. "He's a good boy."

"Yes, he is."

"See you on Friday, AJ."

"Thanks for introducing yourself, Desi. I look forward to working with you."

Kyler returned with boxes of Count Chocula and Frankenberry, his eyes daring her to make him choose only one.

This was a *pick your battles* moment. She patted his shoulder. "Those are better choices anyway."

AJ wiped the flour from her hands and turned off the timer when it started to ding. She pulled two pans of cupcakes out and loaded two new pans into the oven. Squinting at the clock, she realized it was nearly midnight as she reset the timer.

Lord, it was hot in here.

The stairs creaked and she glanced over when Cord lumbered into view. Barefoot, shirtless, his sweatpants hanging low on his hips, his hair disheveled... the man was sexy as hell. He cracked a yawn. "Baby doll. You ever comin' to bed?"

"I just put the last two dozen in to bake. Then I'll be up."

His bleary-eyed gaze roamed around the kitchen and the dining room. Every surface was covered with cupcakes. "I can't believe you baked two hundred and fifty cupcakes in one day. Bet you're glad to be done."

"These aren't done *done*. I still have to frost and decorate them all."

He groaned. "I know you said you didn't want help, but darlin', call my mom. She'd love to lend a hand."

AJ shook her head. "I got this."

"Why you bein' so stubborn?"

"I'm not. This was my idea. It's up to me to see it through." She sauntered forward and grabbed the waistband of his sweats to tug him closer. "But I will let you help me on Friday."

"Doin' what?"

"Hauling the haybales into the school." She smoothed her hands up his torso, making a little purring noise as her fingers coasted over muscled contours of his abdomen and chest. "You should definitely give your fan club a treat by wearing a sleeveless flannel shirt over a super tight T-shirt as you're sexily manhandling the bales. Bonus points if you're wearing Wranglers that highlight your very fine cowboy ass. *Extra* bonus points for donning your dress Stetson."

"Jesus, AJ. You been tippling while you been down here bakin'?"

She laughed and noticed his cheeks had a tinge of red at the mention of his fan club. "I get drunk on you quite frequently, McKay."

He ran the backs of his knuckles down the curve of her jaw. "You're in a mood."

"Seeing you half-nekkid always puts me in a good mood."

"Yeah? How long before you gotta pull them cupcakes out?"

"About eight minutes."

"Gives me plenty of time." Cord grinned. "You've been workin' so hard, you deserve a treat."

Her belly rolled. "I promise I'll be up in ten minutes."

He put his mouth on her ear. "Now."

"Kyler—"

"Is snorin' in his room with the door closed. Come on."

"But—"

"That's one."

Seemed her husband was in a mood too.

Cord threaded his fingers through hers, towing her out the French doors onto the deck. The cool night air felt heavenly. Then he pressed her against the outer wall and took her mouth with unrestrained hunger.

Demanding and teasing kisses coupled with his wandering hands only added to the feverish sensation of her skin. He slipped his thumbs inside the waistband of her flannel lounge pants and slowly pushed them down until they pooled around her ankles. After his fingers connected with her bare ass, he chuckled in her ear, sending goosebumps cascading across her exposed skin. "Glad to see that goin' commando has rubbed off on you, baby doll."

"No panties *is* handy when your man is a total sex fiend."

He bit her neck in that spot and she gasped.

"It is humbling that *my wife* begs her sex fiend husband to do all sorts of dirty things to her, all the time."

AJ loved how much Cord emphasized *my wife* at every opportunity.

Then he lowered to his knees and lifted her left leg, wrapping her thigh around the back of his neck and settling his mouth over her core. Groaning with possession when he discovered how wet and ready she was for him.

AJ let her head fall back and widened her stance. His oh-so-talented tongue proving once again that he wouldn't need even five minutes to get her off if he set his mind to it. Every lick, every suck, every light swirl perfectly placed.

"Yes. Like that."

The orgasm tore through her in throbbing waves that had her grinding her wet sex against his mouth as she gripped his hair to hold him in place.

Panting, basking in the mind-scrambling moment, she felt cool air hit her swollen tissues when he moved.

Before she even opened her eyes, Cord was on his feet, his hard body plastered to hers, his cock gliding in deep.

He buried his face in her neck as he thrust in and out. "Every time, darlin'. It gets better every damn time."

She whispered, "I know," and clamped her hands on to his tight ass, holding on as his strokes gained speed.

Another climax bloomed on the horizon and she held off until that moment when he found release and they spun into the depth of pleasure together.

Every time indeed.

AJ wondered how long the timer had been dinging when she finally floated back into herself.

He flashed her a smirk before he kissed her. "Told ya we had enough time."

Friday morning, Cord followed AJ into town, toting the four haybales in the back of his pickup while she transported the trays of cupcakes in her truck.

The doors to the gymnasium were propped open. Since AJ wasn't sure where the first graders' booths were located, she waited for Cord to exit his truck so they could scope it out together before they started hauling stuff in.

Although she hadn't convinced her husband to dress as she'd suggested, he still looked like sex on legs; hat shading his eyes, dark stubble on his strong jawline that emphasized the sexiness of his goatee, a navy blue McKay Ranches T-shirt tucked into faded button-fly 501s. She'd had a private chuckle this morning, wondering if he believed he was circumventing women ogling his backside by wearing Levi's. *Wrong move, cowboy.* His ass looked better in those jeans than Wranglers anyway.

Ginny, the room parent, waved them over. "Hey, AJ."

Cord said, "That's where you'll be set up?"

"Looks like it."

"I'll get the first one."

AJ walked over to Ginny. "Great place for your booth." There were right by the main door leading into the gym. "Any backlash about our donation?" she asked.

"No. In fact, Mrs. Hutchins said the other teachers were really happy that each kid would get a cupcake just for coming to the festival and they were more than willing to hand out the tickets in their classrooms."

"Good. I also have cupcakes for the teachers and the rest of the staff."

Ginny gave her a one-armed hug. "You are an angel. Whatever was in those envelopes you brought yesterday was a hit with them too. Thank you. As you can see, the signage is already done."

"Perfect. We can stick the pole in a haybale."

Cord shuffled into view with a bale, moving with the strength and efficiency of a man used to pitching hay. "Tell me where you want this."

"Right in front is fine."

They'd just finished bringing in all the trays of cupcakes when Karen stormed over. "What in the world is this?"

"A cupcake stand."

"SPAT did not approve—"

"Oh, I know they didn't. I wouldn't dream of undermining all the hard work the various committees have done for SPAT's contribution to the Festival."

"That's certainly what it looks like," Karen snapped.

AJ pointed. "Go ahead and read the sign before you jump to the wrong conclusion."

Autumn is a season to share the bounty.
Mrs. Hutchins' 1st grade class invites EVERYONE
to exchange a ticket for a cupcake!

"Everyone?" Karen said, spinning away from the sign. "You have two hundred cupcakes?"

"Two hundred and fifty, actually. It's a participation prize. It's important to foster goodwill among all students. Mrs. Hutchins' classroom's theme is *sharing is caring*. Since I didn't have any duties for SPAT, I volunteered to make the cupcakes."

"All of them? By yourself?"

"Yes."

Cord moved to stand beside AJ. "That's what comes from bein' young and full of energy. Our house sure smelled good while she was bakin' up a storm. Sorry to interrupt, darlin', where do you want the rest of them haybales?"

"I'm not sure." She paused and said, "Forgive my rudeness, Karen. This is my husband, Cord McKay. This is Karen...gosh, I'm drawing a complete blank on your last name. But she's the president of SPAT."

"I'm Karen Souther."

"Pleasure to meet you, Mrs. Souther. Forgive me for not shakin' hands. I tend to get a little dirty. Especially when I'm with my wife."

Do not blush.

"That's ah...fine. I'll send Mary over. She's on the decorating committee."

"If she's decorating, she'll be easy enough to track down. I'll leave you to it."

Point for Karen that she didn't turn around and watch Cord swagger away.

Mrs. Hutchins hustled up, her focus on Karen. "Karen. You'll be getting a formal thank you from the teachers, but I just wanted to say what a wonderful surprise that SPAT gave every teacher a voucher for a thirty-minute massage at AJ's studio, Healing Hands. It's all we've been talking about this morning."

Karen flashed her teeth at AJ. "Yes, her generosity was certainly a revelation to us all."

After Mrs. Hutchins left, Karen studied AJ for several long moments.

Somehow, she didn't fidget.

Then Karen said, "Clever, AJ McKay. I'll give you that."

"Thank you."

"If your intention was to prove you'd be a valuable asset to SPAT, you've done that too."

Karen turned and walked off.

AJ smiled. "Bet you won't have a hard time remembering my name now."

Amy Jo McKay

Unicorn Cupcakes

Root Beer Chicken

Root Beer Baked Beans

Buffaloed Brussels Sprouts

Stuffed Pork Loin

Flank Steak Philly Rolls

RECIPES

UNICORN CUPCAKES

1 box vanilla cake mix

3 eggs

½ cup butter, softened

1 cup milk

Blue, purple, and pink food coloring

Pastel sprinkles

Preheat oven to 350 degrees. Line muffin pan with white cupcake liners. In a large bowl, add the cake mix, eggs, butter and milk, and stir until combined. Divide the batter evenly into 3 bowls. Add 10-12 drops of food coloring to each bowl to make blue batter, purple batter and pink batter. To fill the cupcake pan, add one tablespoon of each color of batter to each muffin tin. Bake for 18-20 minutes. Allow to cool completely. When the cupcakes are cooled, remove the center of the cupcake using a teaspoon. Fill with sprinkles, then pipe on the frosting. When you bite into the cupcake you will have a unicorn worthy SURPRISE!

Frosting

4 cups powdered sugar

2 sticks butter, softened

1 teaspoon vanilla extract

2-3 tablespoons milk

Blue, purple, and pink food coloring

In a large bowl, combine all ingredients except food coloring. Divide into 3 bowls and add 10-12 drops of food coloring in each bowl to make blue, purple and pink frosting. Add each color of frosting to a piping bag.

ROOT BEER CHICKEN

1 teaspoon garlic powder

1 teaspoon onion powder

1 tablespoon salt

1 teaspoon pepper

1 teaspoon brown sugar

1 teaspoon paprika

1 4-5 pound whole chicken,
neck and giblets removed

2-3 tablespoons olive oil

1 can of root beer

Preheat grill to 350 degrees using indirect heat. In a small bowl, combine the garlic powder, onion powder, salt, pepper, brown sugar, and paprika. Rub the chicken with olive oil and coat with the spice mixture. Cut the top of the root beer can off and pour out some of the root beer, leaving ¾ of the liquid in the can. Lower the chicken onto the can so that the chicken is upright and the can is in the cavity of the chicken. Place the chicken on the side of the grill without the burners on (this is the indirect heat method). The can and the legs should keep the chicken stable and upright. Close the lid and grill for 1-1 ½ hours or until the internal temperature is 160 degrees. Remove the chicken with the can still in place to a large cutting board. Allow to rest for 10-15 minutes. Using tongs or 2 forks, carefully lift the chicken off of the can of root beer. Discard can and slice chicken.

ROOT BEER BAKED BEANS

2 cans cannellini beans, drained

1 can chili beans, drained

1 cup root beer

½ cup ketchup

¼ cup brown sugar

¼ cup apple cider vinegar

1 tablespoon Dijon mustard

1 teaspoon chili powder

1 teaspoon salt

1 teaspoon pepper

3 slices bacon, cooked and crumbled

1 sweet onion, diced

Preheat oven to 350 degrees. In a large bowl, combine all ingredients. Pour into a 9 x 13-inch baking dish and cook for 45 minutes.

Note: This can also be made in a slow cooker on low for 2 hours.

BUFFALOED BRUSSELS SPROUTS

20-24 Brussels sprouts, cut in half

1 (8 ounce) block blue cheese

8 slices bacon, cut in thirds

1 cup buffalo wings sauce

Preheat oven to 400 degrees. Take one half of a Brussels sprout and place about ½ teaspoon of blue cheese on cut side. Place the other half on top of the blue cheese and wrap the entire Brussels sprout with bacon. Place seam side down on a parchment-lined baking sheet (with sides). Roast for 30-40 minutes or until crispy. Toss in buffalo wings sauce before serving.

STUFFED PORK LOIN

4 tablespoons olive oil, divided

2 slices bacon, chopped

6 ounces brown mushrooms, thinly sliced

⅓ cup onion, chopped

1 teaspoon salt

1 teaspoon pepper

1 teaspoon minced garlic

¼ cup fresh chopped parsley

1-2 pound pork tenderloin

Preheat oven to 400 degrees. In a large oven safe iron skillet over medium heat, add 2 tablespoons oil and cook bacon until browned, 3-4 minutes. Add mushrooms and onion and cook, stirring often, for 5 minutes or until soft. Season with salt, pepper, garlic, and parsley. Cook one more minute, stirring constantly, then transfer to a plate. Cut a slit all the way down the long end of the tenderloin, making sure not to cut all the way through. Open the tenderloin like a book, cover with a sheet of plastic wrap and pound with the flat side of a meat mallet until ½ inch thick, without tearing through the meat. Spread mushroom mixture evenly over the surface of the tenderloin, leaving ½ inch on all sides. Roll tightly, starting with the long end, and secure the ends with 6-7 toothpicks. Poke toothpicks through parallel to each other to create a flat cooking surface. Season all over with salt and pepper. Heat the same skillet over medium heat and add 2 tablespoons oil. Once oil is hot, place tenderloin in the skillet and sear about 2 minutes on all 4 sides, 8 minutes total. Transfer the skillet with the tenderloin to the oven and bake at 400 degrees for 18-20 minutes or until a thermometer reads 145-150 degrees in the thickest portion of the meat. Transfer to a cutting board, brush with the pan drippings, and rest 10 minutes before slicing into rings. Brush with pan drippings for more flavor, then serve.

FLANK STEAK PHILLY ROLLS

2 tablespoons butter

1 sweet onion, thinly sliced

1 green bell pepper, thinly sliced

6-8 button mushrooms, thinly sliced

2 tablespoons soy sauce

1 teaspoon pepper

1 teaspoon garlic powder

2 pounds flank steak

1 teaspoon salt

1 teaspoon pepper

9-10 slices provolone cheese

2 tablespoons oil

In a large skillet over medium heat, add the butter and allow to melt while spreading across the entire skillet. Add in the onion, bell pepper and mushrooms and cook for 8-10 minutes, stirring every few minutes. Add in the soy sauce, pepper and garlic powder and cook for an additional 5 minutes. Remove from heat and set aside. Lay the flank steak on a cutting board and rub salt and pepper on both sides. Using a meat mallet, beat the steak all over to help tenderize. Spoon the vegetable mixture over the entire streak and top with the slices of provolone cheese. Starting at the bottom of the steak, roll it up tightly. Place 6-8 toothpicks evenly across the roll depending on size of steak. Slice the steak into 6-8 rolls, cutting in between each toothpick. Heat the oil in a large cast iron skillet over medium high heat. Sear the rolls, 3-4 at a time, on each side for 2-3 minutes. Place on a cutting board or platter to rest for 5 minutes before removing toothpicks to serve.

Note: This is for a medium rare steak. If you prefer your steak more well done, then place in a 350 degree oven for 10-15 minutes.

CHAPTER 2

GRILLED HARD

Macie McKay hung up the phone at the hostess stand. In a zombielike trance, she walked over to the first barstool at the lunch counter and plunked down.

Velma, owner of The Last Chance Diner, shuffled over and stood in front of Macie.

"Girl. You look like you've had a shock. Who was on the phone just now?"

"I...ah...it was..." Macie's head was spinning. She shook it, as if that'd clear it.

"Did you get bad news?" Velma asked sharply. "Please tell me nothin' bad happened to Carter or the boys."

"That call had nothing to do with anyone in my family." Macie glanced up to meet Velma's rheumy-eyed stare. "It wasn't bad news at all. The opposite, in fact."

"Tell me what is goin' on?"

"It'll sound crazy." She exhaled. "Are you familiar with that show on the Food Network, where the man drives around to restaurants all over the country?"

"*Diners, Drive-ins and Dives.* A hot Italian fella...Guy...something or other is the host. Yeah, darlin', I love that show. Why?"

"Because *that's* who called. The producer or scheduler or whoever's in charge of inquiring if we'd be interested in being featured on their show."

Velma's mouth dropped open so far that her dentures clacked.

"Right? That was my reaction too. I'm still in a state of shock. I don't know why they asked to talk to me instead of you."

"Because your name is listed on the website as head chef, not mine."

Chef. Ha. That was a stretch. Macie was a cook—a damn good cook—but to call herself anything else felt as if she was putting on airs.

"Did they say when they'd be here?"

She ran a shaking hand through her hair. "That's the kicker. They're filming midwestern shows so the crew is in Chamberlain, South Dakota right now. Then they're taping at some restaurant in Rapid City, and they'll stop here on their way to Billings." She blew out a breath. "So in four days."

Cursing, Velma shuffled over to the phone, keeping her back to Macie as she made a call.

Macie's stomach dropped. She'd already told the producer they'd do it. What if Velma didn't want her restaurant on the show? But that wouldn't make sense. Businesses featured on Triple D pretty much tripled their income and their foot traffic. Velma had always been eager to work smarter, not harder. When their dinner sales stayed flat, even after a couple of menu changes, Velma was onboard with permanently changing the hours of operation to 5:30 a.m. to 2:00 p.m. and focusing on breakfast and lunch items. Most days Macie was home by three o'clock in the afternoon.

"Fine. See you then." Velma hung up and leaned against the partition. "Okay, that's settled."

"What's settled?"

"I scheduled an industrial cleaning crew outta Gillette to come in tomorrow night and clean this place top to bottom. Course, I told 'em the focus had to be in the kitchen since that's where them TV people will be taping you—"

"Whoa, whoa, whoa. What do you mean taping me? I can't go on TV! I look like I swallowed a damn beach ball." Macie placed her hand on the swell of her belly. McKay baby number three had three months left to gestate but Macie already felt as if she'd been pregnant forever.

You have been pregnant for most of the past four years.

Velma poured them each a cup of decaf before she sat on Macie's left. "You're in charge of the kitchen, Macie. And I'll be blunt. If not for you, this place would've closed down long ago. You brought new life, new ideas and boundless energy to a restaurant that'd barely been limping along. The food they're comin' to showcase are *your* recipes. You are the heart of The Last Chance Diner. It has to be you. Besides, you look cute as a bug pregnant." She winked. "That's probably why your handsome hubby has knocked you up so many times."

"Okay, you convinced me."

"What dishes are you making?"

"I have to pick two signature dishes and call them back tomorrow. I'm guessing it's so they don't have two restaurants cooking similar things in one show."

Velma tapped her fingers on her coffee cup. "They didn't tell you specifically what they'd heard was good eatin' here?"

Macie grinned. "They did mention the waffle fry sliders." That funky, fun item was the best seller on their lunch menu and a big draw for the restaurant.

"Selling so many of them sliders the first year you came to work here allowed us to give this place a much-needed facelift."

She spun around on her stool. The décor was old west meets diner. With flooring reminiscent of the wooden planks in a historic saloon, swinging half-doors into the bathrooms and the kitchen. The booths had been reupholstered in cowhide print, but they'd kept the rustic wood trim and accented it with corrugated metal. Even the pendant lights above the booths had been crafted out of galvanized tin tubs, created by her super-talented husband. It'd also been his idea to hang them from barbed wire and to fashion the lone ceiling fan out of a wagon wheel.

The diner's exterior had gotten a makeover too. A new neon sign, retro 1950s diner style with a bucking horse that jumped. Carter had also crafted an amazing sculpture out of metal scraps that looked like an old trail rider scouring the horizon—as if gauging whether this truly was the last chance.

Macie's generous husband had planned to donate the sculpture, but Velma insisted on paying for it. With the upswing Carter's career had taken in the past few years, that piece had already quadrupled in value.

"Well, squirt, let's narrow down what other dish you're preparing so at least that much will be done before Carter gets here." Velma drained her coffee. "No offense, but you're lookin' puffy. You need to put your feet up tonight."

Right. With a three-year-old and a toddler, she'd only get a break after they were tucked in bed.

Carter McKay lifted Parker out of his car seat and hoisted him onto his hip. Then he reached down for his son Thane's hand and the trio walked across the gravel parking lot toward the front door of The Last Chance Diner.

As usual, Carter avoided looking at the life-sized sculpture he'd created that served as the diner's focal point. While other people marveled over the placement of metal pieces that brought the cowboy to life, all Carter saw were mistakes he wished he could fix. He'd matured as a welder and an artist in the past three years. Thankfully he'd reached the point where he didn't have to include this piece in his portfolio when he was soliciting work.

Not that he'd be soliciting work any time soon. He'd gotten the most astonishing offer earlier today and he couldn't wait to share the good news with his wife.

Thane raced to his mother as fast as his little booted feet could carry him. "Mama, mama, guess what?"

At least Macie was sitting down so Thane didn't bump into the bottom of her belly. "Chicken butt."

Thane giggled. "No, *monkey* butt."

She smiled at him. "I'll get it right tomorrow."

Parker squirmed to be let down, but Carter held firm. The kid still had a goose egg from two days ago where he'd run headlong into the edge of the hostess stand.

Velma patted Thane on the head as she passed by and held her hands out for Parker. "How's my littlest buckaroo today?"

"Mama."

"Ah. Mama's boy."

Macie sent Carter a look, but he shrugged.

As the youngest son with five older brothers, Carter got called mama's boy a lot—and long past the age his siblings should've dropped it. It used to bother him, but now it didn't. Carter bent down and kissed Macie on the lips. "How you feeling?"

"She needs to put her feet up," Velma inserted.

"*She* is perfectly capable of answering for herself," Macie retorted. Her hand dropped to her belly and Carter placed his over the top of it. "Good. He's been mellow today."

Carter's gaze connected with hers. Then narrowed. She had a definite twinkle in her eyes. Had she somehow already found out about his commission? "I know that look, darlin' wife. You've got a secret."

Macie laughed. "It won't be a secret for long, but the most exciting thing ever happened to us today."

"Let's get a cookie while your mama and daddy talk." Velma shifted Parker to her other bony hip and Thane tagged along behind.

"Let's hear the big news."

"We're gonna be on TV!" Macie spoke so fast that Carter had to tell her to slow down. By the time she finished, he was grinning.

"I'd pick you up and spin you around if I could. Instead I'll say, I'm so proud of you, sweetheart. This'll put the diner on the map for sure."

"I know. I'm in happy shock but I don't have time to bask. I've already checked our walk-in freezer and pantry and placed an additional order from our vendors that'll be here Thursday." She sighed. "They're filming on Friday and Saturday. The producer asked me if we could close for regular business on Saturday, but pack the place with our regulars. So it appears the place is super popular. That's when I reminded him that if we asked all the residents of Canyon River, Wyoming to show up, the diner would still only be half full."

Carter brushed her long, dark hair over her shoulder. "Can you trust me with the 'get the diner packed' edict? At least for the half that aren't Canyon River regulars?"

Macie locked her gaze to his. "You're calling your family?"

"Yep. Every. Single. One. Of. Them." He punctuated each word with a soft smooch on her frowning mouth. "I wanna share my beautiful wife's success with everyone who is important to us." He paused. "Speaking of...have you told your dad and Gemma yet?"

"No. I wanted to tell you first."

I know how that goes. But his news could wait. This was Macie's time to shine—god knew she deserved it. "We'd better stop by their place on the way home. I probably need to tell Rafe that I won't be working on anything for the next week so he can get his hours in at the Bar 9." Carter and his father-in-law, Cash Big Crow, job-shared a hired man. Rafe lived on the Bar 9 Ranch and split his time working as a ranch hand for Cash and being Carter's art studio apprentice.

She frowned. "But you have two commissions to finish."

"That's not something you need to worry about, TV star. I'll get them done."

"We could ask Gemma if she'd mind having the boys for a few hours during the day so you can work—"

Carter kissed her to stop her from babbling. Then he framed her face in his hands. "I've got this. A couple of days away from those projects won't affect my future commissions. You need to be fully focused on your TV spot, because it can be a game changer for you."

Those bullshit-detecting eyes of hers narrowed. "There's something going on that you're not telling me."

Tread lightly here, pal. "Our deal has been you work during the day and I take care of the boys. I go to work when you come home. Sounds to me like you'll be here more than you'll be at home for the next several days. I'm tryin' not to be worried about my wife bein' six months pregnant, on her feet for hours on end. Changing up my schedule to accommodate yours is the least I can do to lower your stress level, doncha think?"

Macie turned her head and kissed the inside of his wrist. "You are the best. I'm just nervous. What if I'm awkward and stiff in front of the camera? And I don't even want to think about how fat I'll look."

"Not fat, baby. *Pregnant.* You're beautiful." He traced the edge of her jaw from her ear to her chin. "I've no doubt you'll be a natural."

"You really are the sweetest man."

"You ready to head home?"

"Yes. Let me grab the roast I found buried in the freezer."

"Please tell me you're gonna make your famous rib roast."

She smiled at him. "I know it's your favorite, so we'll have it as our celebratory family meal on Sunday."

"Sounds good. C'mon boys, let's load up."

Macie prepped a lemon garlic chicken and shoved it in the oven. With a couple of hours until supper, she'd insisted that Carter head out to his studio while she and the boys snuggled up on the couch to watch *Toy Story.*

She let her head fall back and closed her eyes, but her brain still churned. They'd stopped at the Bar 9 Ranch to share the news with her dad and his wife, Gemma. The pride in her dad's eyes had given her the courage to ask his opinion about preparing Indian tacos as her second signature dish.

Her father, Cash Big Crow, was full-blooded Lakota Sioux. Macie's mother was white, so in appearance, Macie looked more Native American than Caucasian. But she hadn't grown up on an Indian reservation like her father had. Although she was an enrolled member of the tribe, she didn't want to appropriate a culture that by blood was hers, but by circumstances wasn't.

When Velma had given her free reign in the kitchen, one of the first things she'd done after learning about the significance of the dish, was to create her homage to it. Her dad had hugged her and said he'd be disappointed if she didn't share the recipe for the best Indian tacos he'd ever had.

Macie had relayed that conversation to Carter on the short drive from the Bar 9 to their home. He parked the minivan next to his pickup in the weedy spot between the small trailer they lived in and the barn that served as Carter's studio.

When Carter didn't immediately bail out of the car, she knew he hated seeing his broken-down truck. Finances were tight and they couldn't afford to get the transmission fixed, which forced them to carpool. She didn't mind, but she knew their paycheck-to-paycheck life weighed on him. He proved she'd read him correctly when he muttered, "I cannot wait to see this shitty trailer and that hunk of junk truck in my rearview mirror someday."

The timer dinging startled her, and she realized she had dozed off. She heaved herself off the couch and finished making supper.

When Carter didn't appear after she'd mashed the potatoes and sliced the chicken, she went ahead and fed their sons. Normally she'd poke her head in the barn and call him to come and eat, but she figured he'd gotten lost in his project. Since he wouldn't get to work for the next several days, she let him be.

After supper, Thane and Parker played while she folded the laundry Carter had started this morning. Then the boys had baths, books and she tucked them in bed.

Another hour passed and still no sign of her husband. Grabbing the flashlight, she tromped out to the barn.

The industrial thump of the metal-bending equipment greeted her as she stepped into his studio. Although Carter had opened the hayloft door, the space was stifling, the air heavy with scents of metal and oil.

Carter must've been feeling the heat. He'd ditched his T-shirt, yet he still wore his cut-proof safety apron that covered his front side from his pectorals to his knees.

But the apron left his back totally exposed.

That glorious expanse of male flesh was a sight to behold. The glistening muscles bunched as he maneuvered a chunk of metal in and out of the machine. Every time he switched positions, his biceps and triceps contracted, showing off his thickly muscled arms.

The man had a killer body. Macie leaned in the doorjamb admiring every strong and sexy inch of him. He'd honed those muscles hauling and hoisting rocks, metal and wood for his sculptures or with ranch work when he helped her dad.

And that fine, fine physique was hers anytime she wanted.

She watched him work, waiting for the opportunity to get his attention. Since he operated dangerous machinery, Macie never surprised him. He wore ear protection which prevented him from hearing her and eye protection that prevented him from seeing her. Their agreed upon signal was a quick flip of the lights—after he'd stepped away from his machinery or tools.

As soon as she'd made the signal, he turned around.

As always, it took a minute for him to get out of the zone he drifted into when he created art. The intensity in his gaze lit a spark inside her that rivaled the heat from his blow torch. She loved seeing him this way; dirty, sweaty, completely focused.

Macie really loved when he switched that focus completely to her.

Walking toward her, he removed his metalworking gloves. Then his ear and eye protection. He untied the apron and hung it on a peg. That left him in button-fly 501s and steel-toed work boots—a guise few men could make sexy, but he did.

"I know that look, Macie darlin'."

She cocked her head. "You should because I wear it every damn time I look at you, McKay."

Carter growled. Then his mouth was hungry on hers even as his hands were gentle.

This was the dichotomy of him. Intense and tender. Driven and adaptive. Confident and unpretentious. Strong and soft.

And still he believed *he* was lucky that *she'd* fallen in love with him.

That just proved he had a sense of humor.

It also proved he didn't know his worth as a man, as a lover, as a partner, as an artist, as a father, so it was her joy to remind him every single day that he was everything to her.

Macie broke the kiss and rested her forehead on his chest. "Carter. Come to bed."

Without a word, Carter shut off the studio lights and took her hand, leading her back to the trailer. He paused only to remove his boots and followed her down the short hallway to their bedroom.

Leaning against the door after he'd locked it, he watched Macie undress. As soon as she was naked, he was on her. Propping a pillow behind her back and dropping to his knees.

All she could see over her baby belly was the movement of Carter's head and those beautiful dark blonde curls she loved to run her fingers through. He paused his kissing and swirling licks to say, "Baby, relax. I'll get you there."

"I know. You always do. Just...don't tease. I need this."

A cocky snicker later and she was coming hard against his clever mouth.

Carter still wore that sexy smirk as he ditched his jeans and spread out on the bed.

Macie climbed over him, balancing on her palms as he lifted his hips and slowly pushed his cock in deep. He groaned with bliss, running his rough-skinned hands up the outsides of her calves and over the baby bump between them. He locked his gaze to hers. "You okay?"

"Mmm. But I miss kissing your neck because it drives you wild."

"You drive me wild." He raised his head to kiss across her chest. "Stay like that. Lemme do the work." He canted his hips. Every thrust at that angle abraded her clit.

She spiraled into her second orgasm as he climaxed with a quiet grunt.

They hadn't moved; they were trying to catch their collective breath when the baby kicked the front of her belly with enough force that she gasped. With enough force that Carter felt it against his abdomen.

"Holy shit."

"I don't think he likes us rockin' his house like that," Macie mused.

Carter helped her onto her side and curled himself around her back. "He oughta be used to it by now." He kissed her shoulder. "You are a horny devil this pregnancy." Another kiss. "Have I mentioned how lucky I am?"

She laughed. "Several times." She angled her head so he could kiss her. And he gifted her with her favorite kind of kisses: long and sweet. When she broke away, a bit dreamy-eyed, she whispered, "I love you."

"Love you too, amazin' Macie. Get some rest, darlin'. The next few days are gonna be brutal."

Carter did his best to keep Macie calm and cared for when she wasn't at the diner. He massaged her swollen feet and relayed the antics of their sons since they'd gone to bed hours before she came home. He listened to her fears and frustrations. Shared in her moments of joy.

Yet...he still hadn't shared his good news. Guilt swamped him when she'd caught him staring into space and he'd been forced to tell a little white lie about what was on his mind. He felt guiltier yet when his restlessness kept her awake. But she hadn't been happy to discover he'd snuck out to crash on the couch.

He and the boys had stayed away for the first day of taping. He'd spent a big chunk of the afternoon on the phone with his agent, hammering out the final points of the contract. His agent promised that the organization who'd contracted his services wouldn't release the name of the artist for the project until the following week.

Saturday morning they were all up early. Thane and Parker outfitted in their favorite cowboy duds, while he'd purposely dressed low-key in jeans, boots, his dress Stetson and a black wool sweater that seemed to have shrunk since the last time he'd worn it. But Macie's eyes positively ate him up when she saw him in it, so he kept it on.

The Last Chance Diner parking lot was full. A semi with California plates was parked right next to the building. Macie's dad, Gemma and their kids were already there. Within half an hour of their arrival, Carter's family began showing up. His mom and dad. All his brothers and their families. His sister. His aunts, uncles and cousins from the West side of his family too. If the locals were bothered by the appearance of the loud and large ranching family, they kept it to themselves.

The show's producer, a thirty-something woman who epitomized the California beach vibe, relayed the orders for the day and started escorting groups inside. Carter hung near the back, just in case Thane or Parker decided to throw a tantrum.

Around noon the filming started. The cooks Diaz, Velma and Nick filled the order window with food. The waitresses Misty, Hanna and DiDi delivered the plates. While the TV crew roamed around the room, asking questions of the customers, Carter left the boys with his folks and ducked into the kitchen to see how his wife was holding up.

Macie stood in front of the big industrial mixer dumping in flour while the host talked to her and another film crew recorded. Luckily there was a dish pass-thru he could wait in where he'd be out of the way.

As Macie prepped food, she shared the story of Indian tacos being born on reservations out of ingenuity to stretch government subsidies. And as a native, she paid tribute to that—with her own twists. Then she mentioned that The Last Chance Diner sourced local food first, but they also supported tribes in southwestern Colorado by purchasing from their farm co-ops. Not only did that provide the restaurant with the freshest natural ingredients, it helped an indigenous economy.

If Carter's shirt would've had buttons, they would've busted in that moment of pride for all his wife had accomplished.

Filming lasted all day, but the boys were tuckered out long before the last camera stopped rolling. Carter kept them entertained and out of the way.

Macie brought the host out to meet him as the crew packed up. Carter had a moment of shyness when Macie bragged about him being the artist who'd created the sculpture out front. He'd dutifully answered questions and even took a business card from one of the production assistants who was interested in commissioning a piece for one of the host's many restaurants.

Late in the afternoon, Cash and Gemma hosted a surprise barbecue and bonfire at the Bar 9 to celebrate Macie's big day. Carter appreciated their generosity and for once didn't feel jealous that he and Macie didn't have enough space to host a party themselves. Their time would come—sooner rather than later.

He loved that he got to spend a day catching up with his family. At dusk they all headed back to Sundance, since ranchers rarely got a day off.

Both his wife and his sons were sound asleep the second their heads hit the pillows.

That allowed Carter time to finalize his plans.

Since Macie had cooked her little heart out the past four days, the next morning Carter and the boys made French toast and served it to her in bed.

A little after noon, Carter said, "Come on, we're going for a drive."

Macie scowled at him and muttered, "So much for my nap."

He managed to keep a straight face.

Two miles past the Bar 9, he turned onto a dirt road—a road that just ended. "Everyone out, I wanna show you something."

Thane and Parker bounded across the grassy expanse, stopping every few feet to look at whatever caught little boys' attention in that moment.

Carter threaded his fingers through Macie's, remaining quiet until she couldn't stand it.

"All right, McKay, what in the world is going on?"

"Isn't this place beautiful?"

"Gorgeous. But—"

"The creek is close, so hopefully we won't have to dig far to hit water for a well." He gestured to a stand of pines. "I wish there were more trees, but we can plant them to create a windbreak. Or an orchard."

Macie got in his face. "Carter. For real. Why are we here?"

"Because this, my love, is where we're building our house."

Her eyes widened. "What? Did you buy land and neglect to tell me?"

"No. Your dad loves having us live so close. He and Gemma decided that when we were ready to build a house, we could build it on their land. This is the best spot, doncha think?"

"How will we pay for it?" She groaned. "My dad didn't offer a down payment too, did he?"

"Nope." He paused. "Remember the renderings I submitted for the Jackson Hole Western Heritage Center?"

"Yes. Omigod, did you get one of the commissions?"

Carter braced his hands on her shoulders. "Macie, I got all *six* of them."

"Wait. Is this the commission that pays six figures?"

"Uh-huh. They're paying me six figures...for *each* commission."

She blinked those beautiful hazel eyes at him in utter confusion and whispered, "How is that possible?"

"Apparently the committee didn't believe they'd agree on just one artist's work, so they solicited submissions from a dozen western sculptors. I guess I was the only artist who sent my renderings as a connected theme. They loved that concept. They'll display all six sculptures as an overarching composition of western icons." He paused and shook his head. "I couldn't believe it when my agent called. This is like—"

"The biggest commission of your career." She studied him thoroughly. "When did your agent call?"

Over Macie's shoulder, he noticed their constantly exploring boys had wandered too far away. "Hey guys," he yelled, "come back here."

They spun around and Thane came running, turning it into a race, competitive even at age three.

Macie's hands landed on his cheeks, forcing his focus back to her. "Carter West McKay. *When* were you informed of this life-changing news?"

"Tuesday."

Her jaw dropped. "The same day the Triple D producer called about the TV spot."

"Yep."

"Goddammit, why didn't you tell me? You've had this amazing news...not only didn't *I* know about it, you didn't share it with your family either, did you?"

"Stop grilling me, Macie."

"Then tell me the truth."

His fingers tightened on her shoulders. "I'd intended to tell you on Tuesday afternoon, but then you had amazing news of your own. You deserved to have all the focus, sweetheart. I wanted that for you."

"But at *your* expense. How is that fair to you? God. I feel like the most selfish person on the planet. Let go of me."

"Not a chance." When her chin wobbled, Carter said, "Oh no, no, no, baby, don't cry."

"I hate this for you. You should've been getting kudos and congratulations from your family yesterday. Instead, you watched as they fawned over *me* like... being on TV was a big deal. *You're* the big deal, Carter. How could you let—"

Carter hugged her as close as the baby bump would allow. "You listen to me, Macie McKay. You're always talking about short-term and long-term gains. Think of it this way: your TV spot was our short-term gain. These commissions are our long-term gain. If I complete a sculpture every two months, it'll take me a year to complete the project. And that's *if* everything runs smoothly. So you bet your sweet ass I had no problem watching you shine in the light of your achievements."

"Why are you like this?"

"What?"

"Sweet and bighearted and p-p-perfect..."

"Hey. Remember you called me perfect when you're dealing with my artistic temperament for the foreseeable future."

Macie sniffled. "You *can* kinda be an asshole when you're under deadline."

"See? I rely on you bein' the sweet one to bring me outta my moodiness."

"That is true." Smiling, she wiped her tears. "I'm still mad at you though."

He brushed his lips down her neck. "I have some ideas how I can get back in your good graces."

"I won!" Thane declared, interrupting the moment as he danced a circle around them.

Parker just flopped on the ground and groaned.

Carter crouched down and spoke to their sons. "What would you guys think about living here?"

"Can we get a dog?" Thane asked.

Sneaky opportunist. "Maybe."

"Okay." Then he and Parker started howling and rolling around in the sagebrush like puppies.

Macie took Carter's hand and they walked toward the river, making plans for the next phase of their lives together.

SPECIALS

WAFFLE FRY SLIDERS
WITH COWBOY CANDY AND SPICY KETCHUP

SWEET AND SPICY SLAW

COWBOY STEAK WITH GARLIC BUTTER

ROASTED GARLIC MASHED POTATOES

PIMENTO CHEESE TOMATO PIE

BLONDIES

RECIPES

WAFFLE FRY SLIDERS with COWBOY CANDY and SPICY KETCHUP

1 tablespoon butter

½ cup diced sweet onion

1 ½ pounds ground beef

1 teaspoon salt

1 teaspoon pepper

1 teaspoon garlic powder

1 bag frozen waffle fries

4 cups oil for frying

*3 thick slices pepper jack cheese,
   cut into 4 squares*

6 slices bacon, cooked and drained

¼ cup mayonnaise

1 cup Spicy Ketchup

1 cup Cowboy Candy

In a small saucepan over medium heat, melt the butter then add the onion. Cook until tender, about 10 minutes. Remove from heat and cool completely. In a large bowl, combine ground beef, salt, pepper, garlic powder and onions. Make into 12 small slider patties. In a large grill pan over medium high heat, place 6 patties (spaced out so they can sear and not steam) in the pan and cook on each side for 3-5 minutes or until patties are well done (internal temperature of 165 degrees). During the last minute of cooking, place 1 square of pepper jack cheese on each patty. Remove from pan and place on paper towels to drain. Repeat with remaining patties. In a Dutch oven or deep fryer, heat oil to 350 degrees and fry the waffle fries according to package directions, then drain on paper towels. To build the sliders, place one waffle fry on a plate then top with Spicy Ketchup, burger patty with cheese, half slice of bacon, Cowboy Candy, a touch of mayo and more Spicy Ketchup. Top with another waffle fry to finish. Repeat with remaining ingredients. Serve immediately.

Spicy Ketchup

1 cup ketchup

2 tablespoons hot sauce

1 teaspoon chili powder

½ teaspoon cayenne pepper

Mix all ingredients in a small bowl and refrigerate for at least 4 hours before serving.

Cowboy Candy

20-25 jalapeño peppers

1 cup apple cider vinegar

3 cups sugar

1 teaspoon ground turmeric

1 teaspoon celery seed

Slice each pepper into ¼ inch slices and discard the stem. In a large pot over medium heat, add the vinegar, sugar, turmeric and celery seed and bring to a boil. Reduce heat to low and allow to simmer for 5 minutes. Return mixture back to a boil and add in peppers. Allow to boil for 30 seconds then reduce heat to low and simmer for an additional 5 minutes. Remove from heat and, using a slotted spoon, transfer peppers to jelly jars (8 ounce). Once the peppers have been removed from the pot, place the vinegar mixture back on the burner and turn heat to medium. Boil for 5 minutes. Ladle syrup into jars with peppers, leaving ½ inch headspace. Place in refrigerator for up to 3 months.

SJ note: The Cowboy Candy is best after 1 week in the refrigerator, BUT if you are like me (very impatient), waiting a total of 1 minute is totally legal in my book!

LJ note: Can I just say hot damn! So so good!

SWEET AND SPICY SLAW

½ cup apple cider vinegar

¼ cup honey

¼ cup olive oil

2 tablespoons hot sauce

1 teaspoon red pepper flakes

1 teaspoon salt

1 teaspoon pepper

1 bag tri-color slaw

In a large bowl, whisk together all ingredients except the slaw. When well combined, add in the slaw and toss to cover. Refrigerate for 2 hours before serving. Can be made the day before.

COWBOY STEAK WITH GARLIC BUTTER

A cowboy steak is a thick-cut ribeye where the rib bone is frenched so it extends out a few inches from the meat for presentation purposes. The typical cowboy ribeye will be 1 ½ to 2 ½ inches thick and weigh 18-36 ounces each.

1 Cowboy Steak

Salt

Pepper

1 tablespoon minced garlic

1 tablespoon softened butter

Preheat a charcoal grill to 350 degrees. The charcoal flavor is important for this cut of meat. Place the hot coals on the left side of the grill. The steak should be at room temperature before starting. Season the steak liberally with salt and pepper (don't be shy...the meat needs it). In a small bowl, combine the minced garlic and butter, then spread on both sides of the steak. Place the steak on the right side of the grill for indirect heat cooking. Grill for 15 minutes on each side, then place directly over the hot coals to sear the steak for 1-2 minutes on each side. Place on a large platter and tent with foil. Allow to rest for 10 minutes before slicing. This ensures that all of the juices will stay with the steak and not end up on the platter.

Add more garlic butter to the steak before serving and I can guarantee any cowboy will tip their hat to you! -SJ

ROASTED GARLIC MASHED POTATOES

1 head garlic

2 tablespoons olive oil

8 baking potatoes, peeled and quartered

1 stick butter, softened

½ cup milk

2 tablespoons mayonnaise

1-2 tablespoons salt

1 tablespoon pepper

Preheat oven to 350 degrees. Cut the top off the head of garlic and place cut side up on a sheet of tinfoil. Pour olive oil on top of the garlic and cover tightly with foil. Place on a cookie sheet and bake for 1 hour. Remove from oven and allow to cool. When the garlic is cool enough to handle, squeeze the entire head into a small bowl, leaving only the skin in your hand. Stir and press the roasted garlic with a fork until smooth. In a large pot of boiling water, add a teaspoon of salt and the potatoes and boil for 15-20 minutes or until tender. Drain potatoes and place in a large bowl. Add the butter, milk, mayonnaise, salt and pepper. Add more or less salt to get to your desired taste. Add in the roasted garlic and blend with a hand mixer for 2-3 minutes until smooth and fluffy.

PIMENTO CHEESE TOMATO PIE

5-6 Roma tomatoes, sliced

1 teaspoon salt

1 deep-dish pie crust

¼ cup diced sweet onion

1 teaspoon pepper

1 batch Pimento Cheese

Preheat oven to 375 degrees. Line a baking sheet with paper towels and place tomato slices in a single layer. Sprinkle with salt to remove excess moisture. Bake pie crust for 10 minutes. Firmly press the tomatoes with additional paper towels to remove as much liquid as possible. Place the tomatoes in the bottom of the pie shell and sprinkle with onions and pepper. Spread the pimento cheese evenly over the tomatoes. Reduce heat to 350 degrees and bake for 30 minutes.

SJ note: Cowboy Candy (page 41) is a great addition to this dish to add that "boot with a spur" kind of kick.

Pimento Cheese

1 (4 ounce) jar pimentos, not drained

8 ounces shredded white cheddar cheese

8 ounces shredded yellow sharp cheddar cheese

1 tablespoon garlic powder

1 cup mayonnaise

In a large bowl, stir all ingredients until combined. Refrigerate for 2 hours to overnight to allow flavors to come together before serving.

BLONDIES

2 sticks butter, melted

1 ¼ cups light brown sugar

½ cup sugar

3 eggs

1 teaspoon vanilla extract

2 ¼ cups flour

1 teaspoon baking powder

1 teaspoon salt

⅔ cup white chocolate chips

1 cup chopped pecans

Preheat oven to 350 degrees. Line a 9 x 13-inch pan with parchment paper and spray with nonstick spray. In a large bowl, combine butter, sugar, eggs and vanilla until smooth. Gradually add in the flour, baking powder, and salt. Stir until smooth. Fold in the chocolate chips and pecans. Pour into prepared baking dish and bake for 25-30 minutes or until a toothpick inserted in the center comes out clean. Allow to cool before slicing.

CHAPTER 3

LONG HARD BOIL

Colby McKay was pitching hay for the horses when a big Dodge truck barreled up his driveway.

At first, he thought his older brother Cord had come calling, because the man drove like an idiot. He squinted at the driver—while telling himself he did *not* need glasses—and realized his sister-in-law AJ was behind the wheel of Cord's truck.

She hopped out. Then his other sisters-in-law, India and Domini, exited the passenger side and the trio started toward him.

Leaning on his pitchfork, he drawled, "Happy as I am to see you all, Channing ain't here. She took the kids to the dentist in Spearfish."

"We know," AJ said. "We wanna talk to you."

Jesus. He did not like the sound of this. "Okay. What's goin' on?"

"Channing hits the big four-oh next week. Are you doin' anything special for her?" India asked.

Colby pushed his hat back. "I hadn't really thought about it."

Sweet, usually shy Domini spoke next. But not to him: to India and AJ. "See? This is why we need to do this."

Both AJ and India nodded.

"Do what?" Colby asked.

"Throw a surprise fortieth birthday bash for her," AJ said.

He took a moment to organize a response instead of blurting out *that's a terrible idea.* "While it's really thoughtful of you all to wanna do this for her... surprises ain't really her thing." Ah, hell. That was a really frickin' lame answer.

"And how would *you* know that? Have *you* ever thrown her a surprise party?" India demanded. "Have you or your kids *ever* planned a surprise for her?

You stepped into that one, buddy.

Colby made a show of looking around for someone who wasn't there. "Where's my sister? This sounds like one of her schemes."

"That's just it, Colby. The responsibility for special occasions in the McKay family shouldn't always fall on Keely's shoulders," Domini said softly.

"So this is basically a courtesy call," India said. "We *are* havin' a big party for Channing next Friday night."

No sense in arguing then. "You just need me to...what? Get the kids ready, acting as if we're takin' her out for supper? Then we'll meet up with you and everyone else where you're hosting the party?"

AJ, India and Domini exchanged a look and then laughed. A laugh that sounded slightly evil. "This isn't a family party. This is just for us girls," AJ said. "We need you to tell her on the morning of her birthday that you're gifting her an hour-long massage. We'll take it from there."

"Wait," Domini said. "Maybe Colby has a point about convincing her that he and the kids will pick her up after the massage and take her out for supper. That way she'll have clothes to change into. She wouldn't be happy if she showed up to her surprise party in yoga pants and a ratty T-shirt."

"True. Then after we get her to the party venue, we'll tell her you were in on it and that you're takin' care of the home front while she's enjoying her birthday night."

"Any questions?" India asked.

"Not that I can think of right now. Except...you're *sure* this is something Chan will like?" Meaning: *she won't get pissed off at me for agreeing to it.*

"If she isn't having fun, someone will bring her home. Cool?"

Colby nodded.

"You'd best be thinkin' about buyin' a present for her too, Mr. 'I Haven't Thought About It,'" AJ warned.

He kept his mouth shut instead of retorting *I know.*

"If there's a change in plans on your end, text one of us. We'll do the same."

"Thanks for keeping this quiet," Domini said.

The trio had nearly reached AJ's truck when Colby said, "If this is ladies only, then there won't be male entertainment?"

No response.

Fuck. That didn't bode well.

Well, at least they hadn't left him with another round of evil laughter.

Colby had the table set and the food ready to dish up when his boisterous brood barged into the kitchen.

"*Dad* cooked?" their oldest son, Gib, said.

"I thought we were outta fish sticks," second oldest son, Braxton, said.

Colby snorted. He was a little handier in the kitchen than heating up frozen food.

"I don't care what it is," Miles, their third son, said. "I'm *starvin'*."

"Me too," added Austin, the youngest boy.

Talia, his only girl, elbowed her brothers aside to reach him. "Daddy, I gotta surprise to tell you about."

Must be the day for it. He swooped his daughter into his arms and kissed her forehead. "Where's your mama?"

"I'm here," Channing said, pausing in the doorway.

If he'd seen this dark-haired beauty on the street, with her sparkling eyes, generous smile and tempting curves, he wouldn't have believed she was nearly forty. After almost a decade and a half together, she still lit up a room—and his heart—whenever she walked in.

"Heya, shug."

"Heya, yourself." Then she said, "Huh-uh, boys. Wash up first, then you can come to the table. You know the rules."

"Aw, man."

Talia squirmed to be let down, always wanting to be in the thick of things with her brothers.

"And one of you help your sister," Colby said, loud enough for the boys to hear.

He pulled Channing into his arms and planted a kiss on her mouth. "How'd it go?"

"Fast, considering they saw all five kids today. It's a cool space. Lots to keep kids entertained while they're waiting for their turn in the chair."

"I hate that now you have to go all the way to Spearfish instead of just into Sundance."

Channing tucked a piece of hair behind her ear, but it immediately fell forward again. Last month, claiming she needed a change, she'd chopped off her long, dark hair. The shorter style brought out her natural curl, and looked fantastic, but she still hadn't gotten used to those curls continually falling into her face. "I'm happy to make the drive. I would've sat in Dr. Benton's office for hours or had to make several trips. Plus, this dental group is right next door to the orthodontist."

Colby's eyes searched hers. "What'd they say?"

"For now, it doesn't look like Gib will need braces. But Braxton will. Thankfully, we'll have a couple of years to save up for that." She smiled. "Thanks for getting supper ready."

"You're the one who made it—which I'm sure the kids will be happy about. All I did was turn on the oven."

She stopped at the sink and washed her hands. "Any issues today?"

"Nope. It's always fun drivin' a Bobcat. I got the first layer scraped away. Chet and Remy stopped by to check my progress. But I really think they just wanted to make sure I hadn't been screwing around with their machine."

"The boys will be so excited," she murmured and squeezed his arm.

Since it appeared his sons were determined to follow in his steps competing in rodeo events, he decided to plat out a dedicated dirt arena for them to practice in. His dad had done it for him and his brothers, and it'd given him an advantage. If Gib and Braxton had their way, they'd be ropin' and ridin' from sunup to sundown, so at least they'd be close by when they wanted to practice.

Then the kids raced back into the kitchen, ending their conversation.

Later that night when they were in their bedroom, Channing was engrossed in something on her laptop. Something that put a frown on her face.

"Everything okay?"

She glanced up at him. "Just...fretting over styles."

"C'mere. Lemme see."

"No. It's fine. I know it's been two weeks but I'm still having a hard time choosing."

"Chan. Come to bed. Bring your laptop."

"All right." She switched off the overhead lights and turned on the lamp on her nightstand before she sat cross-legged on the bed.

Colby stretched across the mattress, his head close to her hip so he could see the screen. "What am I lookin' at?"

She sent him a smirk. "You can't tell these are building plans? You need to get your eyes tested, old man."

"Fuckin' hilarious."

"I know you've seen these three final options fifty times, but I don't know which one looks better. Like your cousins told us, adding another addition onto a log home has challenges. The amount of space we gain is nearly identical with all three. So it is down to aesthetics." She sighed. "It'd be easier if you'd weigh in."

He refused to give an opinion on which rendering he preferred. It'd increase their living space and that's all that mattered to him. Besides, she'd already discarded his secret favorite because it added considerably more square footage and cost more money. "You really aren't leanin' toward one in particular?"

"They're all good. I think maybe...since we don't need a nursery anymore that we should put this expansion project on hold." Bent over her computer, her hair covered her face so completely he couldn't see her expression.

But he felt her pain. That punch of sadness he'd become familiar with in the past few months since she'd lost their baby. Channing still struggled and he didn't know how to help her.

Colby reached over and gently closed the laptop.

She set it on the nightstand and scooted down until she was tucked against his side. "I'm sorry. I'm sure you're sick of hearing about it."

He tipped her face up to stare into those sorrow-filled hazel eyes. "You know better than that, Chan. A loss is a loss. I ain't about to tell you to get over it."

"I know. And I wasn't accusing you of anything." She curled her hand around the side of his face. "You've been amazing, Colby. Understanding. Patient and loving..."

They shared a bed every night. He held her every night. But they hadn't been intimate since before the miscarriage. He missed that physical connection—and likely she did too—but he'd never push her to resume that side of their relationship. She'd give him a sign when she was ready.

Absentmindedly, Channing trailed the backs of her fingers up and down his jawline.

"What?

"I'm serious about holding off on starting the addition."

"That is not an option. We're in the West Construction queue and for all I know, it could be two years before they could fit us back into their schedule. We still need the space, shug, sooner rather than later. Regardless if one of the new bedrooms becomes a nursery."

"Then I want you to choose a design. I'm done obsessing over it."

"Done."

She shifted away to turn off the lamp.

When she kept her back turned toward him, Colby spooned in behind her. "If I'm picking the exterior design, does that mean I get to pick the interior too?"

A snort. "Nice try. And let this be your warning I'm putting a moratorium on antlers used as décor."

"Doesn't look like Dewey's is open," Channing said over her shoulder to AJ, who was standing behind her. "Are you sure Colby planned to meet me here for my birthday dinner?"

"Try the door," AJ urged.

As soon as she swung the door open, the lights came on, confetti floated down and a million voices yelled, "Surprise!"

Channing screamed.

Then amidst noise makers, a chorus of "Happy Birthday" broke out.

After the song ended, her gaze swept over the faces spread out in front of her. Female faces. "I take it I'm not meeting my husband and kids."

"Nope! Girls' night to celebrate the start of your fifth decade," AJ said.

"God, that makes me sound old." Then she placed her hand over her racing heart and said, "You assholes scared every bit of relaxation right out of me."

Everyone laughed.

"Come in, sit down and we'll get you a drink."

Her eyes narrowed on the CLOSED FOR A PRIVATE EVENT that Domini placed in the front window of the restaurant after she locked the door. Her questioning gaze sought out her sister-in-law Keely. "Did you do this?"

"Not me this time," she said cheerfully. "Blame it on AJ, Indy and Domini. With assistance from Macie and Gemma."

Gemma, one of her longtime friends, who lived two hours away, stepped forward for a hug. "You haven't aged a day in fifteen years, girlie."

"You'll go to hell for lying."

More laughter.

Halfway through her round of hugs, AJ brought Channing a drink in a flamingo-shaped glass. "Pink Flamingo. Since you'll ask what's in it...pink-lemonade flavored vodka, cranberry juice, triple sec and a splash of strawberry seltzer."

"Yum. Thank you." She took a sip. "Oh wow. That is good."

"And for the ladies who prefer a nonalcoholic cocktail, we have the Blue Dolphin, which is blue raspberry Gatorade, white cranberry juice and ginger ale."

"That sounds good too." She knew the booze-free drink wasn't only for Indy's sake, but several members of the family were pregnant.

Do not think about that tonight.

It filled her with gratitude that nearly all the McKay cousins' spouses were here. Kade and Kane's wives, Skylar and Ginger. Brandt and Tell's wives, Jessie and Georgia. As well as Quinn's wife, Libby, and Ben's wife, Ainsley. Also in attendance was Gavin's lady, Rielle, Chassie, from the West side of the family, plus Channing's friends Brooke and CoCo.

It seemed strange the McKay matriarchs weren't here.

Keely must've noticed her looking for them because she said, "My mom, Aunt Kimi and Aunt Vi are on standby as extra DDs tonight if we need them."

"Plus, we didn't want them around if we decided to bitch about their sons," India added.

Macie gave India a considering look. "Do you want to bitch about Colt?"

"Hell no. But since *I've* got the perfect McKay, I figured the least I could do was listen as the rest of you complained about yours."

Boos rang out. Sweet Jessie even balled up a couple of napkins and tossed them at India.

"Besides," AJ inserted, "someone needs to bail us outta jail if need be."

Domini whirled around. "We cannot get arrested tonight!"

"Why? Is Cam on duty?" Ainsley asked.

"No, he's home with the kids."

"So we're in the clear. Wahoo!" Keely said with a fist in the air. "Let's crash karaoke night at the Twin Pines after we eat cake."

Channing shook her head. "Do you not remember the cops breaking up fistfights, and you getting permanently banned from there?"

"Then you spouted off to Cam and he nearly tossed us all in the slammer," Libby said.

Ginger laughed. "I could've talked my way out of that for all of us."

"Says the lawyer," Skylar said dryly.

"Sounds like we missed some fun," Brooke remarked to CoCo.

"Yes, the wild days are behind us," Chassie remarked.

"Thank goodness," Libby chimed in.

"Oh, pooh," Keely scoffed. "I, for one, will *not* let motherhood change me."

That cued the loudest laughter so far.

AJ signaled for their attention. "Enjoy the appetizers, but keep in mind that Macie and Domini prepared a feast for us tonight. Now...who needs another cocktail?"

Music provided a happy groove. Channing made the rounds, laughing, talking, drinking, having a good time getting her buzz on.

When mealtime came, they seated her at the head of a long table.

Dinner consisted of three courses. The first was an arugula salad with beets, goat cheese crumbles, pistachios and a tangerine honey dressing. Course two was a plate of small beef croquettes, served atop roasted garlic couscous with a side of spicy, quick-pickled purple cabbage.

Channing panicked for a brief moment when AJ said, "Speech time."

Keely stood. "Chan, thank you for being the first woman to agree to put up with one of my dumb brothers for longer than one night. After being the only girl on the McKay side, with the multitude of...maleness, I was thrilled to finally have a sweet, sassy sister. We're all here because we love you. Raise your glass for a toast...to Channing!"

Maybe Channing had too much to drink because she felt a little teary-eyed. But thank god there weren't any more speeches.

After the dinner plates were cleared, Domini took the floor. "When we were planning this party, we refused to make the theme anything related to you being *over the hill*—this is a celebration of the years that shaped the woman you are and of all the great things to come for you." She paused. "That said...we have to poke a little fun. So the last dish, is a traditional celebration treat I had growing up in the Ukraine." She walked forward and placed the ramekin in front of Channing.

Her eyes narrowed. "Domini. Are these...prunes?"

"Why, yes they are."

Channing took one bite and immediately talked with her mouth full. "These are amazing. What do you call them?"

The foreign word rolled off Domini's tongue, but Channing didn't attempt to repeat it.

"Translated, that means they are prunes stuffed with walnuts and topped with sweetened condensed milk."

"Go ahead everyone and dig in," Channing urged. "And fair warning, Dom, you *are* bringing these to the next McKay family party."

Drinks were refilled and the party took on a low-key vibe...until a shrill whistle ended the chatter.

Everyone looked at India.

"Okay, ladies. Who can't follow instructions? We specifically said NO GIFTS in the invite." She held up the offending package, wrapped in a plain brown wrapper and tied with twine. "Who did this?"

No one fessed up.

Then Gemma said, "Well, the gift is outta the bag, so I think she oughta open it."

A chorus of "open it, open it" started.

India presented it with a flourish.

Even after Channing ripped the wrapping off, she wasn't quite sure...

"Let us see."

AJ, the closest one to her, read the box text out loud. "Remote controlled vibrating butt plug—a gift your man will be buzzing about for days!"

Keely snickered. "I'd love to see the look on Colby's face when you whip that out during sexy times."

"Can't you just hear Channing? Bend over baby," Ainsley cooed, "it'll only hurt the first time."

"Or...I'll only put the tip in, if you don't like it...well, too fucking bad," Domini said in a perfect imitation of Cam.

Then it was a goddamned free for all. Channing couldn't remember the last time she'd laughed so hard.

Someone cranked the music. Someone else started dancing and then they were all singing and dancing to the "girl power" playlist. Booze flowed. Laughter echoed.

When a lull hit, India and Gemma served lemon cake and coffee.

Despite being tipsy, Channing had to share her gratitude before people started to leave. "Well, you put on a helluva surprise party. I never imagined I'd be part of a family like this. My McKay sisters, and my friends, I'm blown away by the love you show me, so thank you, because it means everything to me." She took a sip of her Irish coffee to moisten her suddenly dry throat. "I've...ah...I kind of closed down after my miscarriage. Along with the physical pain, my emotions whiplashed all over the place, from *get over it* to *I deserve to wallow*. As I look across this room, and see all the important women in my life, I realize, I don't know how many of you have ever dealt with the same thing."

She paused, trying to stem the rising tide of feelings, but she just let them flow rather than bottling them up again. "How wrong is that? How stupidly wrong is it that losing a pregnancy is still something women don't talk about to each other? As if it's contagious or something to be ashamed of or something to feel guilty about. Then I feel guilty because whenever anyone whispered 'miscarriage' around me, before I knew the devastation that word means, I avoided the person dealing with it.

"When it happened to me, I didn't unburden myself on anyone except for Colby. While I love him down to my soul, and he is an amazing father, and was as supportive as he knows how to be, the life inside of me doesn't become real to him until the screaming baby arrives as proof. So loss doesn't affect him the same way." She sniffled. "I'm not trying to be maudlin, it's just easy to gloss over the bad things when good things outweigh them. I wanted to apologize for not being there for any of you the past few months."

Even before she sat back down, Jessie said, "I, for one, appreciate your honesty. I lost a baby when I was married to Luke. And yet, that didn't prompt me to reach out to you when I heard your sad news, and for that, *I* am sorry. The only way to change this mindset we all seemed to have about discussing miscarriage, even in this day and age, is if we agree to talk about it. To each other. To our daughters. Yet, I think we've all been burned by judgment of other women. Obviously, no one in this fabulous group, but the nasty comments linger and make it hard to put yourself out there, so I understand why you pulled back into your safe place to heal."

"But that leads me to the question...why do some women suck so much? I mean, what gives them the right to comment that I'm too damn old to have babies?" Gemma asked.

"Or when they sneer at you for being too young and an unwed teenaged mother," Rielle added.

Domini nodded. "Or when they snarkily comment that you sure have a lot of kids and are all of them really yours?"

"Or when they keep askin' when you're gonna start a family, not knowing that you've been trying for years to do just that," Libby said.

"Or when you decide parenthood is not for you," Ainsley said, "and they try to convince you if you had a child, it'd change your mind."

"Or when you opt to only have one child and they say it's a pity the kid will grow up lonely," CoCo said.

"Or when your same-sex partner isn't considered a 'real' parent even when she's been there from conception to birth and every day after," Brooke said.

Skylar leaned forward. "Or when your children are all girls and they ask when you're gonna try for a boy."

"Or when people point out you're not the kid's 'biological' parent," AJ said, "as if I should treat him differently."

"Yes!" Ginger said. "Like your spouse can't love the child you brought into the marriage as much as the children that come after."

"Or when people rudely ask your child's ethnicity, as if that's their right to know," Macie said with a huff.

Chassie groaned. "Damn, ladies, I thought all this kinda bullshit was directed at our family because we're poly, with mixed ethnicity, but I hate to hear that you've all dealt with this nastiness."

"Oh, show up to preschool covered in tattoos and you'll hear some nastiness about your 'fitness' as a parent," India scoffed.

That's when Keely burst into tears. Immediately Georgia was by her side, offering tissues and consoling her.

Horrified, because Keely never cried, Channing said, "Are you okay?"

"No. Hormones." She dabbed her tears. "I'm mad that anyone in this room has had to defend or explain or justify *any* of the life choices they've made, especially to other women. And I hate that if I hadn't heard these issues that you've all dealt with, that maybe I'd be one of those women. So I wanna thank all of you for keepin' me, a soon-to-be first-time mom, from bein' a judgmental dick."

That eased the tension. Then everyone was hugging and crying and laughing. It was a potent affirmation and reconnection.

Channing felt...freer. Sharing her burden had lightened her load.

While she loved this female friendship and empowerment love fest...she had a love fest of her own to tend to. Another declaration of intent. Another promise to keep to the man who soothed her and protected her. Colby had been patient and sweet...but she was finally ready to reacquaint herself with her husband's hunger. Revel in his passion that existed solely for her. Bask in the heat of his physical intensity. Relish his raunchy side. Glory in his possessiveness that made her feel like the sexiest woman alive.

Once they'd exhausted themselves renewing their sexual shenanigans, she planned to kick up their kink a notch with her new birthday gift.

Right after she'd sexted Colby her dirty thoughts to get him pumped, Gemma said, "Let's do some shots, birthday girl."

Gib was still awake when Colby received Channing's text. Thankfully, the other kids were in bed, so he told his oldest to stay alert in case they needed something.

Alone in his truck, he couldn't help but chuckle at how she'd worded her text.

I need to ride you home.

Twenty minutes later, Colby parked in the empty lot down the block from Dewey's.

Women were shouting goodbyes from the front of the restaurant as others headed to their cars. He couldn't make out their faces—not because he needed glasses—but due to darkness.

Sure, buddy, keep telling yourself that.

When he stepped into the restaurant, he noticed the only people still hanging around were his sisters-in-law and... "Kyler? What the devil are you doin' here?"

"Dishes. Me 'n Anton are getting paid to clean up."

"You've done this before?" What he meant was...*ain't you a little young?*

Anton tossed Kyler a rubber apron. "Hey, Uncle Colby. I'm familiar with the dish machine since I work here on weekends. Could probably load it in my sleep."

That reminded him these boys were nearly young men now. In a couple of years Gib could get a job here. Talk about feeling old—and it wasn't even his birthday. "It's good of you guys to help out."

"Our moms volunteered us."

"Oh. Well, have you seen my wife?"

Then he heard, "*There's* the perfect McKay, ladies. You all can suck it," and turned to see Channing practically skipping toward him.

He loved witnessing her wide smile and the happiness shining in her eyes. "Hey, darlin'."

"Heya, my big, sexy cowboy." She twined her arms around his neck. "I'm happy that you came to get me but...I wasn't supposed to text you."

"I'm glad you did, birthday girl." Colby kissed her, tasting some sweet liquor on her lips. "Did you have a good night?"

"The best. I've never had a surprise party, and I was so frickin' surprised I actually screamed. Wasn't it super sweet and thoughtful of my McKay sistas to do this for me?"

"Yep." He'd forgotten how damn cute a tipsy Channing was. The ride home oughta be interesting. "You ready to go, shug?"

"Uh-huh." Sighing, she pressed her body closer to his. "Have I mentioned how much I love the sexy tone of your voice when you call me that? Still gives me tingles."

"Tingles are good."

"Mmm." She kissed his chin and murmured, "Say it again. I've missed that tingly feeling. A lot."

Colby looked into her eyes and the lust he saw reflected back at him stirred more than his blood. "Me too. But maybe this ain't the place to talk about it?"

"Good idea." Channing dug her fingers into the back of his neck, tugging his face closer to whisper, "But here's a better idea. Let's skip the talking entirely and get straight to the action—hot, dirty, naked action."

"Chan—"

"Ah-ah-ah. Say *shug* all low and growly like a beast. It gets me so hot. Like everything inside me is ready to boil over."

Jesus.

Then she flicked the brim of his Stetson. "Yep. I'm gonna want you totally nekkid ASAP...except for this hat. Been a while since we've played ride 'em cowgirl."

Oh for fuck's sake. He was gonna have a goddamned hard-on in front of his brothers' wives and he'd never live that shit down.

AJ walked over with India right behind her. "I'd planned on giving her a ride home, but she said she texted you."

Colby shifted Channing so she stood in front of him. "Looks like you've got your hands full cleanin' up. Is there anything you need before we take off?"

"Nope. Here's her backpack with her purse, change of clothes and her...ah... birthday gift."

India snickered. "Yes, that gift caused quite a buzz."

Christ. Of course they'd given her a vibrator.

Better that than them hiring a male stripper to give her a lap dance.

"Well, at least it sounds like a gift we'll both enjoy."

AJ, India and Channing busted a gut laughing.

Whatever. Colby settled the strap of her backpack over his shoulder. "Just in case my hammered wife forgot to say it, I will; thanks for the party."

"Hey, buddy, I'm not hammered." She smirked. "But a good pounding is what I'm hoping for to end my birthday right." Channing winked at AJ and India.

"And...we're out."

Keeping his arm around her waist, Colby guided them outside, while trying to dodge her flailing hands as she waved goodbye to everyone.

This part of main street was quiet; he could hear the western music and drunken revelry echoing from the bars up the street. Felt like ages since they'd been out on a Friday night.

Somehow, he misinterpreted Channing's sudden stillness as weariness. But as soon as they were in the building's shadow, she pounced. Pushing him against the brick, plastering her body to his, connecting their mouths in a frenzied kiss. Her busy fingers were untucking his shirt from his jeans and then scraping her nails up his back. She moved her mouth down to bite his neck. "I missed you. I missed this." Then her fingers were yanking on the button of his jeans. "I need you to fuck me."

"Chan—"

"Colby. Don't you remember when you were so fucking hot to bury that big cock of yours inside me that you banged me outside a bar, in a laundromat, and against the horse trailer?" She panted against his neck. "Let's relive those wild times. Fuck me. Right here, right now."

As much as it pained him to do so, Colby circled his fingers around her wrists, stopping her wandering hands. If those clever little fingers touched his dick, he'd forget why this was a badly timed idea. "Yes, I wanna be up in you so goddamned bad my balls ache, but not here."

When her shoulders slumped and she dropped her head to his chest, he growled, "Shug. Look at me."

She tilted her head back. Horny as it made him to see lust—not the haze of alcohol—clouding her eyes, he had to tread lightly. "I will fuck you hard and fast at home. Up against the wall in our bedroom, in the shower, hell, even on the floor in the damn barn. But after not touchin' you for a few months, I'll need to take you in our bed first. You can pick where we start the second go around." He brushed his lips across hers. "And the third. And the fourth. I don't wanna rush what I've been lookin' forward to because some drunken fool is comin' around the corner to take a piss."

A beat passed and she sighed. "Point taken. I'll press pause...but I reserve the right to fondle you in the truck on the way home."

"I'd expect nothin' less from you, hot stuff."

COWBOY BITES

$\mathcal{C}$hanning's head throbbed.

    Throbbed.

Christ on a cracker, it'd been an eternity since she'd been this wrung out.

She gingerly turned her chin, trying to find a softer spot on the pillow.

Ooh. Mistake. That hurt her neck.

The hard thump of the bedroom door closing had her groaning.

"Mornin', love." She felt Colby's weight as he perched on the side of the bed and set something on the nightstand.

Then the alluring scent of coffee teased her.

"C'mon, darlin'. You know you wanna wrap your hands around it and drink it down. But you've gotta sit up first."

"Fine, demon man." Channing rolled over and sat up quickly, hoping the movement would be like ripping off a bandage.

Whoo. Yeah. Not doing that again. Her midsection ached as if she'd done two hundred sit-ups last night.

Then Colby's callused hands wrapped her fingers around the cup of life-affirming ambrosia. She lifted it to her mouth—ouch, goddammit, even her lips were sore—and she swallowed two big gulps.

"Demon man?" he repeated. "I'm hopin' that's because I was a demon in the sack last night."

Images of heated bodies in motion, echoes of whispered words and lovers' moans rolled over her, and through her, sending new shivers dancing across her skin. He had made good on his promise to bang her everywhere until she practically passed out from sheer sexual bliss.

"You're lookin' a mite...ragged."

She squinted at him. He was smirking. "I'm blaming my love hangover on you, cowboy."

"Love hangover?"

"We both know I wasn't drunk when you picked me up after the party, but you definitely got me sex drunk with that...depraved cock of yours."

Colby laughed. "*Deprived* cock, you mean. It missed you." Tenderly, he brushed her hair out of her face. "And baby, you were the one who kept saying *harder-faster-more-more-more* because we were makin' up for lost time."

"Using my sex-induced delirium against me? Nice, McKay."

"You ain't really complaining...are you?"

The concern in those stunning blue eyes, that maybe he had gone too far, had her reaching for him and stroking his jaw. "No. Like I said last night, I missed that part of us. I'm relieved that it was easy to get back in the saddle—so to speak. Thanks for being so patient."

"Baby, you're the one who taught *me* patience." Turning his head, he kissed her wrist. "I love you. We're in this for the long haul. And uh...remember that patience thing when you see what the kids have done to your kitchen while makin' you a belated birthday breakfast."

Fab at 40

Buffalo Chili with Spicy Cornbread

InstaPot Bacon Ranch Chicken Pasta

Bacon Wrapped Quail

Not So Grilled BBQ Ribs

Venison Chimichangas

Homemade Crescent Rolls with Honey Butter

Caramel Apple Upside Down Cake

RECIPES

BUFFALO CHILI WITH SPICY CORNBREAD

1 teaspoon oil

1 teaspoon butter

½ cup diced onion

2 tablespoons tomato paste

1 pound ground buffalo*

2 tablespoons chili powder

1 tablespoon cumin

1 teaspoon paprika

½ teaspoon cayenne pepper

1 teaspoon salt

1 teaspoon pepper

1 (15 ounce) can chili beans

1 (28 ounce) can crushed tomatoes

In a large pot over medium heat, heat oil and butter. Add onion and cook until tender, about 5 minutes. Add tomato paste, stirring to combine. Add ground beef and cook until no longer pink. Drain fat and return to heat. Add chili powder, cumin, paprika, cayenne, salt and pepper. Add chili beans and crushed tomatoes and bring chili to a boil. Reduce heat and simmer 20 minutes.

*Ground beef may be substituted.

LJ note: I'm so happy that Suzanne included game recipes in this cookbook!

Spicy Cornbread

½ cup oil, divided   *1 ⅓ cups milk*

2 cups self-rising yellow cornbread mix   *1 teaspoon salt*

1 egg   *½ cup diced, pickled jalapeños*

Preheat oven to 450 degrees. In a large cast iron skillet, pour ¼ cup of oil and spread to cover the bottom. Place in the oven for 5 minutes. In a large bowl, combine the remaining ¼ cup of oil and the other ingredients. Pour into hot skillet and return to the oven. Bake for 15-20 minutes or until golden brown.

INSTAPOT BACON RANCH CHICKEN PASTA

6 slices bacon, chopped

3 tablespoons butter

4 cups chicken broth

½ cup heavy cream

1 packet ranch seasoning

16 ounces penne pasta

2 boneless, skinless chicken breasts, cut into 1-inch pieces

8 ounces cream cheese, cubed

1 cup shredded sharp cheddar cheese

Turn on the Sauté function on your Instapot. Add the chopped bacon. Cook, stirring occasionally, until done. Remove and place on a paper towel to drain. Remove the excess grease from the pot. Add the butter and a little bit of the broth to the pot and stir, scraping the bottom of the pot so you can to get up all of the brown bits/goodness. Add the remaining broth, heavy cream, and ranch seasoning, then stir well. Add the pasta and stir. Add the chicken and the cubes of cream cheese. Don't stir, but gently push down, using a spoon, to submerge the chicken and pasta. Cancel the Sauté function. Place the pressure cooker lid on the pot and turn the steam release knob to the Sealing position. Press Pressure Cook or Manual button, and then the + or - button to choose 5 minutes. When the cooking cycle ends, do a controlled Quick Release of the pressure, just until you are sure no sauce will spew out with the steam, then turn the knob all the way and let it all out. Open and stir the chicken and pasta. It will be soupy at this point. Stir in the cheddar cheese and bacon. Mix well and allow to thicken for 5 minutes before serving.

BACON WRAPPED QUAIL

12 quail breasts*   1 tablespoon minced garlic

2 jalapeños, sliced   1 teaspoon dried sage

½ cup soy sauce   6 slices bacon, cut in half

½ cup honey

In a large resealable bag, place quail breasts, jalapeños, soy sauce, honey, garlic and sage. Close bag and massage to cover quail with marinade. Refrigerate for at least 4 hours to overnight. Preheat oven to 450 degrees. Remove breasts and jalapeños from the marinade and place one of each on a slice of bacon. Wrap the breasts with bacon and secure with a toothpick. Place on a parchment-lined baking sheet and drizzle remaining marinade over the breasts. Bake for 20 minutes.

*May substitute boneless, skinless chicken breasts cut into 2-3-inch pieces.

NOT SO GRILLED BBQ RIBS

2 - 2 ½ pounds baby back ribs

1 teaspoon salt

1 teaspoon pepper

1 tablespoon olive oil

¼ cup finely diced onion

1 teaspoon ground cumin

½ cup ketchup

1 tablespoon Sriracha

2 tablespoons light brown sugar

1 tablespoon apple cider vinegar

Preheat oven to 275 degrees. If the ribs still have the thin membrane covering the back of the rack, remove it. Season both sides of the ribs with a generous amount of salt and pepper, then place meat side up in a large roasting pan or rimmed baking sheet. (It may be necessary to cut the ribs in half to fit them in the pan). Cover the pan or baking sheet tightly with aluminum foil, and bake for 3 to 4 hours until the meat is tender and falls off the bone. While the ribs are baking, make the barbecue sauce with the remaining ingredients. In a saucepan over medium heat, add the oil and allow to get hot. Add the onions and cook until soft and translucent, about 10 minutes. Stir in the cumin and cook for an additional 30 seconds. Add the ketchup, Sriracha, brown sugar, and apple cider vinegar. Stir to combine, season with salt and pepper, then cook for 2 more minutes. Set aside for the ribs to finish cooking. Remove the ribs from the oven and generously brush both sides with the barbecue sauce. Turn broiler to high and broil the ribs for 3-4 minutes, just until the barbecue sauce begins to caramelize.

VENISON CHIMICHANGAS

6 cups oil for frying
1 pound ground venison*
½ cup diced onion
1 (15 ounce) can tomato sauce
1 packet taco seasoning
1 cup shredded Monterey jack cheese
1 cup shredded sharp cheddar cheese
1 jar pickled jalapeños or Cowboy Candy (page 41)
1 egg
8 flour tortillas

Heat oil to 350 degrees in a Dutch oven or deep fryer. In a large skillet over medium heat, cook venison until no longer pink; drain. Return venison to the skillet and stir in the onion, tomato sauce and taco seasoning. Simmer for 8-10 minutes on low. Spoon about ⅓ cup of beef mixture off-center on each tortilla. Fold edge nearest the filling up and over to cover. Fold in both sides and roll up. Whisk egg and brush it over last part of tortilla to seal. Fasten with toothpicks. Fry the chimichangas for 1 to 2 minutes on each side or until browned. Drain on paper towels. Sprinkle with cheese and top with jalapeños.

*May substitute 1 pound ground beef.

HOMEMADE CRESCENT ROLLS WITH HONEY BUTTER

½ cup warm water

1 tablespoon quick rise yeast

1 teaspoon sugar

⅓ cup sugar

½ cup softened butter

½ cup warm milk

1 egg

1 teaspoon salt

4 cups bread flour

In the bowl of a stand mixer, stir together the warm water, yeast and sugar. Allow to sit for 5 minutes. Add in the remaining ingredients and mix with the dough hook attachment on low until a dough forms. Remove from bowl and place on a lightly floured surface. Knead for 2-3 minutes, then place in a clean glass bowl that has been wiped down with oil. Cover with a cloth and allow to rise for 1 hour. Remove the dough from the bowl and cut in half. Roll out one portion of dough into a 10-inch circle. Using a pizza cutter, slice the dough into 8 triangles. It will resemble a sliced pizza pie. Roll each triangle into a crescent roll by starting with the wide end and rolling toward the point. Place on a greased cookie sheet and allow to rise for 30 minutes. Bake at 350 degrees for 10-12 minutes. Serve with Honey Butter.

Honey Butter

1 stick butter, softened

1 tablespoon honey

Combine the 2 ingredients in a small bowl. Place on a sheet of plastic wrap and roll into a cylinder. Refrigerate until hardened. Slice as desired.

CARAMEL APPLE UPSIDE DOWN CAKE

¼ cup butter

⅔ cup dark brown sugar

2 apples, peeled, cut into ½-inch wedges

1 box spice cake mix (I use Betty Crocker)

1 cup water

½ cup oil

3 eggs

Heat oven to 325 degrees. Spray a 9-inch pan with nonstick spray. In a small saucepan over medium heat, melt butter and stir in brown sugar. Bring to a boil then remove from heat. Pour caramel into the 9-inch pan and spread evenly. Lay the apple slices evenly over the caramel. In a large bowl, mix together the cake mix, water, oil and eggs until blended. Pour over apples and spread to cover. Bake for 1 hour or until a toothpick inserted in the center comes out clean. Run knife around sides of pan to loosen cake. Place heatproof serving plate upside down over pan; turn plate and pan over.

CHAPTER 4

ALL JAMMED UP

"What am I supposed to do with two bushels of peaches?"

Keely McKay Donohue glared at the four baskets packed to the brim with fuzzy fruit.

While she appreciated the thoughtfulness of her sweet mother-in-law, Doro, carting these "early beauties" back from Colorado because she'd gotten a killer deal on them—this was an abundance of riches. *Half* of the original abundance since Doro had showed up with four bushels.

Keely had shared with her family, her friends, her kids' friends, her coworkers and PT clients...until they'd started asking if everything was "just peachy" anytime they saw her.

Bunch of smartasses.

But her normally sainted mother reigned as smartass queen supreme, because she'd retitled the super-secret recipe for her peach preserves...*We Be Jammin'.*

Now every time Keely glanced at the recipe card, she got that stupid song stuck in her head.

Still...she wished her mother was here right now.

Normally if Keely's mom wasn't around to help out, she could call her mother-in-law. Or her aunt Kimi. Even her aunt Vi. But no. They'd all loaded up for a road trip to a George Strait concert...after they'd collected four cases of pint jars, dropped them off and wished her luck as "All My Ex's Live in Texas" blared from the convertible Doro had rented.

She refused to contemplate what mischief the four of them would get up to without any "menfolk" around as they ogled and *whoo-hooed* King George.

Keely heard singing from the den, where her kids were engrossed in another viewing of their favorite Disney flick, *Aladdin*. Good. That gave her a little time to call in reinforcements.

Pulling up her contact list, she called her best friend, AJ, who was also married to Keely's oldest brother, Cord. She hit the icon for the speakerphone and wandered to the fridge to snag a diet soda as the line rang.

AJ answered with, "No."

"You don't even know what I'm gonna ask."

"Yes, I do."

"Okay, smarty-pants. Then tell me."

"You've put off dealing with all that fruit, hoping someone would rescue you and now it's just one day away from being overripe and you're desperate for help."

Dammit. "I'll let you dance around me singing 'I told you so' and give you half of the damn jam if you come over and keep me from screwing it up."

"No deal. My kids are away—"

"What? All of them?"

"Yep."

"Where'd they go?"

"To my sister's in Montana. Ky had football camp, so my mom and Jenn suggested all the kids come up and stay for two weeks."

Keely frowned. "Why didn't I know this?"

"Because I knew if I told you, you'd assume I had nothin' better to do than jam with you."

Jesus. The puns were getting out of hand.

"Besides, we won't be around."

"We? Meaning you and Cord?"

"Yes. We're actually taking a vacation. We're leaving tonight after chores."

She didn't ask who'd be dealing with their livestock, because the McKay Ranches Company employed enough family members that each of them had a chance to take a break if needed. "Where are you going?"

"An adults-only, all-inclusive resort in Jamaica!" AJ squealed. "Cord set it up as a surprise. Isn't that just the sweetest thing?" She sighed. "Hottest thing, more like. Just my man, the sun, the sand for an entire week. Pretty much all I'm packin' are swimsuits, sunscreen and extra lube."

"Eww. TMI. That's my brother you'll be ridin' like a seahorse."

AJ laughed. "We've been married long enough that you should be used to me waxing poetic about my studly husband."

"Whatever. Have a great time. Don't sunburn your titties or your va-jay-jay during your epic sexfest."

"Aw, c'mon, don't be...*jelly*."

Keely groaned. "Hanging up now."

"Love you, Keels. Making preserves is easy and I know you can do it. They won't taste like your mom's, but no one expects that. There's no need to call anyone else to help you get out of this—"

She ended the call before AJ got the "j" word out. Then she paced around her center island before she scrolled to the next name on her list. Her sister-in-law Channing, who'd married Keely's brother Colby.

Once again, she hit speakerphone and listened to the line ring.

Channing answered with, "No."

"God. Sometimes I hate caller ID." She paused. "How do you know what I'm gonna ask?" A suspicion formed. "Did AJ text you?"

Her sweet sister-in-law laughed a little meanly. "I could fake being hurt that I wasn't the first McKay on your call list, but the truth is...I can't help you, even for the chance to peek at Carolyn's secret jam recipe. I'm already elbow deep in canning tomatoes, chopping cucumbers, freezing corn, slicing cucumbers, quartering cucumbers—"

"Fine. I get it. You're overworked and underappreciated."

"Wrong. Colby shows his appreciation frequently. *Very* frequently."

"Eww. TMI. No wonder you two have so many kids."

Another laugh. "Normally, I'd be more than happy to help you *preserve* your sanity, but I'm in a *pickle* myself."

"Omigod, Chan, are you drunk?"

"I wish. I'm sick of cucumbers. I've made three kinds of pickles and I still have a ton left, so I have to get creative. Since Colby is haying, and the kids have a million 4-H projects for the fair, and the older boys are involved in junior rodeo, that means I'm running all over hell and back. Like everyone else in the area, I have a garden that has gone crazy this year with all the rain. So I'm putting up stores between all of these activities."

"I am really sorry that I'm not able to help you."

Channing snickered. "No, you're not."

"Okay, home canning is not my thing. Which is why I can't believe I'm trying to do it without my mom to guide me. What if I mess it up?"

"Honestly, it's the easiest thing to do. Fruit, sugar, heat and time. That's it. Just dive in and get it done. Even when it probably won't taste like Carolyn's, you'll *relish* the results."

"Everyone is a damn comedian. At least it wasn't another jam joke. Good luck, Chan." She hung up.

Keely paced while she scrolled down the rest of her family list. She truly wasn't trying to pass off this chore; she just needed someone—anyone—with canning experience to be her wingwoman. Sure, she'd helped her mom years ago, but she'd mostly been a gopher and she hadn't really paid attention because she never thought she'd need to know the details.

And she was nervous. Maybe it seemed stupid, but her mom's peach preserves were legendary in their family. In the whole damn county. Everyone asked for the recipe and she'd never given it out.

Until now. To her only daughter. A recipe passed down to her from *her* mother.

No pressure.

Her finger paused on the name of her sister-in-law India, who was married to Keely's brother Colt. Then she snorted. Indy, for all her awesome attributes, couldn't cook worth a damn. She'd be a hindrance rather than a help. That was the same reason she skipped over her cousin Kane's wife, Ginger, who was a lawyer. Keely's cousin Bennett's wife, Ainsley, was a banker, and she lamented about her lack of knowledge of being a "proper" rancher's wife, so Keely scrolled past her too.

She paused on the name of her sister-in-law Macie, married to Keely's brother Carter. Pity that Macie lived two hours away. She was an actual cook, with her own restaurant, so could probably craft fabulous jam in her sleep.

Another scroll past her cousin Kade's wife, Skylar. She owned Sky Blue natural beauty projects and she'd just launched a new goat milk-based skin care line, so toiling over another boiling pot probably wasn't how she wanted to spend her weekend.

Speaking of...her cousin Chassie provided the goat milk for Sky Blue products. But with one ranch, two husbands, three businesses and four kids, she had enough on her plate. Keely skipped over her. Ditto for her rancher cousins Quinn, Brandt and Tell. Their wives—Libby, Jessie and Georgia—were likely elbow deep in canning too.

Gavin, her only local McKay cousin not involved in ranching, had married a woman who earned her crust creating home-crafted goodies—everything from spinning wool to selling jars of honey from her hives. Keely knew Rielle would happily teach her the tricks of the trade, but she'd gone to Montana to visit her daughter Rory, so that option was out.

That left Keely down to her brother Cam. He'd joined the sheriff's department instead of the family cattle business, so this was her last option: begging his wife, Domini, with her years of restaurant experience, for help.

The line rang and Keely paced.

Her sister-in-law answered, "Keely! We were just talking about you."

In the background, Keely heard Cam bark, "Tell her no!"

She stuck her tongue out at the phone, reverting to the little sister being tormented by her big brother. "Hi Domini, how are things?"

"Good. Cam and I both have the day and night off from work and you know how rare that is."

She did. And *crap, crap, crap,* that did not bode well for her.

"How are you?" Domini asked.

"Panicked. I have all of these peaches to deal with. I'd love to give you a bushel for the restaurant. No charge. I'll even deliver!"

"While that is thoughtful, peach anything isn't a big seller for us, so I'll have to pass."

"Shoot." Keely sighed. "I don't suppose you'd be interested in coming over to ensure I don't screw up two bushels of peaches when I attempt to recreate my mom's peach preserves?"

"Ah. I don't know. Maybe? I could...just—"

A muffled noise sounded and then Cam spoke. "Heya, sis. Your timing is *uncanny.*"

"Cam. Put Dom back on the phone."

"Nope. I'm stepping in because you're tryin' to ruin my sexy time plans with my lovely wife and she's too accommodating to say *no* to you. You are aware that our *jam-packed* schedule, with half a dozen kids, doesn't give us much time alone."

"Jam-packed. Har har."

"Besides, you know if I'm sending Dom over, the kiddos will demand to come with her so they can play with their cousins. And between our six and your four... do you *really* want ten kids tracking sticky fruit all over your big fancy house?"

Her brother had a point.

"Why isn't your husband helping you can them?"

"Jack had meetings in Denver. He's supposed to be home late tonight or tomorrow."

"Well, there's your answer. Wait until he gets back."

But she'd promised Jack, when he'd given the rapidly ripening baskets of fruit the stink eye four days ago, that she'd deal with the peaches before he returned home.

"But—"

"Great chatting with you, K. Good luck tryin' to replicate Ma's recipe..."

Domini yelled, "You'll do great! I have complete faith in you."

Then the call ended.

Keely stared at her phone. "I have a million goddamned McKay relatives and not *one* of them is available to help me? What kind of bullshit is that? I am so not helping any of them ever again."

"That's okay, Mama. We'll help you."

Keely whirled around. Her five-year-old daughter Piper had snuck up on her. Again. "Hey sweetie. Is the movie over?"

"Almost." The green eyes she'd inherited from her daddy studied Keely in the same manner that Jack did when he was working out a problem.

"What?" Keely said, a bit defensively.

"I'm gonna get Katie and the Things."

She'd given up reprimanding Piper for referring to her three-year-old twin brothers as Thing One and Thing Two, which she'd shortened to just The Things.

Before Keely responded, Piper said, "Be right back," and raced away.

Then the thundering footsteps of her children echoed down the long hallway from the den. JJ, the oldest of their twin boys, was the first into the kitchen, loudly proclaiming, "I won!"

"You cheated," Piper said.

"Did not," he retorted.

"Did too," Katie, her four-year-old said, siding with her sister.

The three of them looked to Liam, the youngest of the twins, to pick a side. But he ignored them and stood in front of his mother, holding up his arms.

Keely hoisted him onto her hip. Then her sweet boy rested his head on her shoulder and sighed.

I know the feeling, buddy.

"Mama? Can we please help you?" Piper said.

"Pretty please?" Katie said.

"Pretty pretty please?" JJ added.

She eyed her kiddos. Piper, the oldest, her redheaded Miss Bossypants, was the ringleader. Katie, her blond-haired dreamer usually had her head in the clouds. JJ and Liam, dark-haired with McKay blue eyes, were identical in looks, but complete opposites in personality. JJ was the loud competitive one, whereas Liam was quiet and contemplative. All so different, but each one wore an expression of eagerness that melted her already soft heart.

"Okay. You can help me."

"Yay!"

Liam squirmed to get down.

"But there are a couple of rules. Making jam requires heat. So the stove will be hot, the pots will be hot, the jars will be hot, and the jam will be hot. I need promises from all of you that you won't mess around in the kitchen—this means no singing or dancing or fighting or running or kicking or karate-chopping or tickling. You don't want to hurt each other, yourselves or me on accident. This requires pinkie swear kinda promises."

The most serious promise in the Donohue household also carried the biggest punishment for breaking it. The kids looked at each other and then each held out their pinkie for Keely to hook into one at a time.

"All right. First we need to wash the fruit. Let's bring the baskets in here."

"I'll get 'em!" JJ cried and took off toward the entryway. Liam trailed behind.

Keely rooted through the dishtowel drawer and pulled out the aprons that her mom had sewn for the kids, as well as piles of towels.

As soon as Katie had her apron on, she started twirling as if she'd donned a ballgown.

JJ huffed back into the kitchen, lugging the basket of fruit nearly the same size as him.

"Careful," Keely warned...just as JJ bobbled and dumped half the fruit on the floor.

Deep breath. Bruised peaches didn't matter at this point.

"Sorry, Mama."

"I *told* you that you'd drop it!" Piper said as she and Liam skirted the fruit pile and set the second basket on the floor by the sink.

"Katie, there's no dancing in the kitchen when we're making jam, remember?"

"Oh. I forgot." She did one final pirouette and her foot landed on a runaway peach, squashing it. But apparently the pit dug into her arch, causing her to yell, "Owie!" and she fell onto her bony little butt, on top of two more peaches.

"You okay?" Keely asked.

"Uh-huh. The peaches are smooshy."

"I know, sweets. That's why we've gotta get the jam done. Can you help JJ pick up the peaches that were dropped?"

"You mean the peaches that *JJ* dropped because he never listens to me," Piper corrected.

"You're not the boss of me, *Piper,*" JJ shot back.

Keely tuned out their bickering. After putting the plug in the enormous farm sink, she gently tumbled in one basket of peaches and started to fill it with warm water. By the time JJ and Katie had all the peaches picked up from the floor, the bobbing fruit was level with the countertop.

"What's that for?" Liam asked when Keely returned with the padded bench from the entryway.

"You're all going to stand on it *very carefully,* no pushing, no shoving, no elbowing, no fighting, and wash the peaches while I get the other stuff ready."

"Let's have a race," JJ said, hopping up on the bench. "Bet me'n Liam can do more than you two."

"Bet you can't," Piper retorted, and she and Katie jumped up beside them.

"THERE WILL BE NO RACING EITHER."

JJ sighed and muttered something to Liam.

Keely didn't want to know what that was about. "We are a team and we'll work together. It doesn't matter who is fastest or first." How many times a day did she have to repeat that? "You all wanted to help me, remember? So it's—"

"Mama's way or no way," Katie chirped.

"That's right. Now see the towels I've set on the counter? That's where you'll place the peaches after you take them out of the water." Keely retreated to her walk-in pantry to retrieve the sugar, pectin and jar of candied ginger—which was her mom's first secret ingredient, not fresh ginger. Secret ingredient number two was lime salt—homemade, of course. But Keely had cheated and ordered hers online.

As she rooted around for an extra roll of paper towels, Liam walked into the pantry. "Mama? You got any more scrub brushes? Piper and JJ won't share."

"What in the world do they need scrub brushes for?"

"To scrub the fruit."

"Good lord, no, I did not tell them…" Crap. She hadn't given specific instructions for them *not* to scrub the fruit. Gathering up her supplies, she shooed Liam out of the pantry. After setting everything on the counter, she walked through the puddles to the sink.

Peach pulp and skins floated on the surface as JJ and Piper attacked the fruit with vegetable scrubbers. "Stop. The peaches do not need to be scrubbed with a brush."

"But we scrub potatoes like this. Carrots too," Piper said.

"Peaches are delicate. You're tearing them apart."

"Then how're we 'sposed to wash 'em?" JJ asked.

"Gently. You're basically getting them wet to get rid of any dirt or leaves or bugs."

"Bugs? Eww," Piper said.

"Maybe there's worms in some of 'em too," Liam said hopefully.

"Mama, I am not touching worms!"

"I doubt there are any worms, Piper. Just roll the peaches around in the water and then put them on the towels. That's all you need to do."

Keely brought the boxes of jars and the two giant canning pots into the kitchen. She also snagged three of her own pans to cook the jelly. Good thing she had a six-burner stove.

While the kids washed the fruit, she measured out dry ingredients. Tempting to double the recipe and save herself half the cooking time, but she already had enough misgivings about how this jam would turn out. She spread two layers of parchment paper on the work surface and taped it down.

Then she heard *blub blub blub* followed by giggles and looked over to see JJ plunging his face into the sink. Then Liam did it. Then they all four laughed.

"JJ and Liam. *What* are you doing?"

"Bobbing for peaches! It was my idea to practice for the school carnival."

Seriously? This kid was already giving her gray hair and he was *three*. "Stop. That's just...gross. And now you're all wet. Go take off your shirts."

The boys raced away, their sisters followed, whispering back and forth.

Keely eyed her kitchen. The floor in front of the sink was sopping wet. She hadn't cleaned up the smooshed peaches yet...and how would she ever get all this fruit cut up? It'd take hours. For a brief moment she considered handing the kids plastic knives to help her, but that'd likely result in a visit to the emergency room.

Panic swamped her. She slid down into the corner space between cupboards, legs curled into her chest floor and closed her eyes.

Too much noise. Too hot. The smell of the peaches and sugar was too sweet. She couldn't get enough air into her lungs. Her clothes were wet and clinging and constricting and she just wanted to scream.

Deep breath, buttercup.

I'm trying.

Throw the damn peaches away if you're gonna get this upset about it.

She scoffed at Jack's voice in her head. *I'm not upset.*

Yes, you are. This is supposed to be fun.

It is not even close to fun, GQ. It is super stressful.

Find a way to make it fun for them and less stressful for you.

How?

Relax. Everything will be a mess so don't get hung up on that. It'd be a mess even if the kids weren't helping you.

She sort of hated that he was right. *Okay.*

So what if it's not how your mom does it. It's how you do it. The kids just want to be a part of it. You're making more than jam, babe. You're making memories with them. That's what matters.

Cue her lightbulb moment.

The boys bounded past her, without shirts because she hadn't specifically told them to put on clean shirts. But truthfully, fruit wouldn't stain their skin, so it was a smart move.

She rolled to her feet. "Listen up. Before we get to the next part, we need clean clean hands."

Clean clean was a level above "kid" clean. They knew the drill. They lined up and Keely used a disinfecting wipe on each set of hands.

"Mama? How come the Things don't gotta wear shirts?" Katie asked. "It's not fair. I don't wanna ruin my pretty apron from Gran-gran."

Keely started to say that being shirtless was okay for boys...but how sexist was that? Teaching her girls that they had to cover up, as if the upper portion of their bodies were somehow shameful. Fuck that. They were kids. They were in their own house. What did it matter if they all went shirtless? "Katie, sweets, if you want to take off your shirt, go ahead. Same for you, Piper."

The girls doffed their shirts like it was no big deal.

Keely clapped her hands together. "This is the best part." She moved the bench to the center island. "Two of you get to stand, two of you sit on the chairs. Figure out who is where—without arguing." She dumped the peaches on the parchment paper.

"What do we get to do now, Mama?"

She grinned. "Smash them." To hell with cutting them all in perfect little cubes. She sliced a peach in half, scooped out the pit and set the halves down in front of Piper. "Go ahead. Squash it."

"Really? I won't get in trouble?"

"Not even a little bit. Go for it."

Piper placed her palms flat on the fruit and pressed down. She giggled. "That is ooshy gooshy."

"Let me try, let me try" echoed around her.

Almost as fast as Keely halved and pitted the peaches, the kids were mashing, smashing and squishing. And having a grand old time doing it.

There was no way this jam would turn out like her mom's and for the first time all week...she didn't care. Laughter and giggles were the sweetest balm to her nerves. Every time she cracked open a jar, *this* is what she'd remember.

Piper scooped the mash into the measuring cup and Keely dumped it in the pan. Wasn't long before she had all three batches of jam going. The kids didn't lose interest in their smash and grab until nearly all the peaches were pulverized and mounded in bowls that stretched across the marble countertops.

"Mama?"

She glanced up at Piper. "Yeah, sweetie?"

"This is so fun. Can we do it again?"

"Yeah! We should take all of these pits and plant them," JJ said. "Then we'd have millions of our own peaches!"

Liam enthusiastically agreed.

Only Katie was the hold out. "What's the matter, honey? You're not having fun?" she prompted.

"I am. I just wish Daddy was here."

"Oh, baby. Me too."

And as if conjured by the wishful thoughts of his wife and children, a suit-and-tie-clad Jack Donohue waltzed into the kitchen, threw his arms open and said, "Who wants to give Daddy a welcome home kiss and a squeeze?"

J ack didn't notice until after he'd tossed out the invite that his kids were covered in peach goo. He squinted at JJ; the boy had chunks of fruit glistening in his hair.

All four children stopped their activities and ran toward him.

Maybe he should've changed clothes first.

Crouching down, he braced himself to accept their sticky hugs and sweet kisses.

"Daddy, we're helpin' mama make jam!" Piper said.

"It's the funnest thing *ever*," Katie said.

"I see that." Jack stood when the kids abandoned him. Two steps into the kitchen, his right loafer stuck to the tile. He did not look down when a substance squelched around his left loafer. He kept a steady pace toward his wife.

Three pans of jam bubbled and two enormous, blue-flecked canning pots boiled. She glanced up from stirring and smiled at him. "We were just talkin' about how much we wished you were here. And here you are. Although, your attire is a tad fancy for our jam session, GQ."

Jack's heart rolled over. This fiery, gorgeous, mouthy, exasperating woman owned him, heart, body and soul. He didn't shy away from kissing her like she was everything to him, because she was.

Before he backed away, he whispered, "Missed you, cowgirl." Then he leaned over the closest pot. "This smells amazing."

"We got to smash all the peaches, Daddy."

"With our hands!"

"As hard as we wanted," JJ added. "It was so cool."

Jack looked at Keely and raised a questioning eyebrow.

"It's true. My little helpers saved me from hours of slicing and dicing. Macerated is macerated no matter how it gets done. It's not like I'm entering the jars in the fair for judgment."

"Look at you and your problem-solving skills, turning a chore into a chance to jam out. I'm impressed."

"That I was able to relinquish control and enjoy the fruits of our labors? Me too." Keely's gaze encompassed the kitchen. "The peaches are prepped but I still have two more rounds to finish."

"You have *six* batches left to make? How much jam do we eat in a year?"

She hip-checked him. "Waste not, want not. Your mother gifted them to us. What else was I supposed to do with them?"

"Uh...Freeze them? I mean, we have an enormous deep-freeze in the garage that's half-empty."

Keely squinted at him. Opened her mouth. Closed it. Her cheeks bloomed red. "I am completely mortified to admit that option never crossed my mind. Between work, the kids, and fretting about screwing this up..."

Then Jack felt guilty. He'd just expected Keely to handle this, with four kids underfoot, while he was in Denver on business. Then again, she had a million relatives around, so he assumed she'd have help. Wasn't the first time he'd made that mistake, but it would be the last.

"I'm sorry I wasn't here to lend a hand when it appears this became a Donohue family activity without any assistance from the McKays." He pointed to the pans of bubbling goo. "How much does that make?"

"According to the recipe, each batch makes six pints, so...I'm prepping eighteen jars."

"I cannot wait to eat our jam, Mama," Katie said.

"Our jam is gonna be the best *ever*," Piper added.

Jack noticed Keely's soft smile at their girls when they said *our jam.*

"Yeah, I'm having two PB&Js every day," JJ declared.

"Me too," Liam piped in.

"See? It won't go to waste. I'll finish this round and do one more batch. Whatever smashed fruit is left over I'll freeze for pies, muffins, or whatever."

"Good." Jack kissed the top of her head. "I was worried you might be making enough to share with your family."

She snorted. "You're familiar with *The Little Red Hen* story. I'll give some to our mothers and my aunts who provided the jars, but that's it."

"So if your helpers are done in here...I was thinking we could have a water fight."

The kids started jumping up and down.

Keely sent him a grateful look. "That sounds like a blast. You guys better head out and get your squirt guns ready for an epic battle with the champion."

Their half-naked tribe of hooligans tore out the patio doors and into the yard.

"Smart move, Donohue. Hosing them off outside before we toss them in the tub."

"It's the least I could do." Jack set his keys, wallet, and cell phone on the breakfast nook. Strange to see the entryway bench in the kitchen, but it was handy. He plopped down and removed his shoes and his socks. Then his tie, and lastly, his belt. He spun around and saw Keely eyeballing him. "What?"

"You tryin' to tempt me by getting undressed in the kitchen?"

He grinned. "Always. But I'm not getting undressed. This might be a *tad fancy for a water fight,* but it's what I'm wearing."

Her expression turned to horror. "Why?"

"The kids will get a kick out of it. It's just clothes. No big deal."

"I remember a time when it would've been a very big deal for you, GQ. So I'm guessing that suit is headed for the dry cleaners," she said wryly.

"Well, there is that too." Jack returned to stand in front of her. Cupping her face in his hands, he said, "I really *am* sorry I wasn't here to help you, buttercup."

She blinked those vivid blue eyes at him. "It's weird, but in a way, you were here. When I started to panic because I knew my kitchen would be trashed, and I worried the kids wouldn't heed my warnings about the dangers of canning, and I beat myself up that my pitiful attempt at making jam wouldn't live up to my mother's standards...your voice in my head is what calmed me down. It was as if you were standing next to me, soothing me, and you literally pulled me up."

He kissed her, the sweet taste on his tongue didn't have a damn thing to do with peaches. The way her body automatically arched into his, fit against his, moved in perfect rhythm with his, fired his lust for her that still burned hot after nearly a decade together.

Keely eased back from their kiss. "I told the kids no screwing around in here, and that includes us."

Jack's gaze searched her flushed face. Feeling smug that her eyes were dark and her breathing had turned rapid. "We'll pick this up later."

"Definitely."

That's when he noticed she had a spot of something on her collarbone.

"What?"

"Hold still." He angled forward and licked it off. Mmm. Peaches. And Keely.

"Jack! What are you doing?"

"Stealing a small taste. You might need to be hosed off later too."

"Ugh. That is an awful euphemism for sex."

"Wasn't a euphemism, because babe, you need a shower." He kissed his way up her neck, stopping at her ear. "You're hot, sticky and sweet in all the wrong places. I'll use my hands and my mouth to get you hot, sticky and sweet in all the *right* places."

"Dirty talker," she said on a breathy moan.

"You love it." He traced the edge of her jaw with barely there kisses. "Can I tell you something else?"

"I love you too."

"That's true, but it's not what I was going to say."

"Oh. Well...better spit it out fast. The kids are waiting for you."

"Waiting to ambush me." He blew in her ear and absorbed her body into his when she went a bit weak-kneed. "You, Keely West McKay Donohue, are totally my jam."

She groaned against his chest. "Seriously, Jack? A jam joke?"

"What? It was funny."

"At least that's one I hadn't heard before." She tipped her head back and stared at him. "But no more."

He grinned. "Not even one about getting you out of your *jammies* later?"

She growled at him and shoved him out the door.

BBQ Pizza with Peach Bacon Jam

Stuffed Meatloaf

Potato Crusted Quiche

Cranberry Chicken and Wild Rice

Southwest Salad with Chipotle Ranch Dressing

Brie and Bacon Cauliflower Mac & Cheese

Confetti Coffee Mug Cake

RECIPES

BBQ PIZZA WITH PEACH BACON JAM

1 refrigerated pizza crust
1 batch Peach Bacon Jam
1 cup of shredded pork (from your favorite place)
½ cup thinly sliced red onion
1 cup shredded extra sharp cheddar cheese

Preheat oven to 425 degrees. On a pizza stone or pizza pan, spread out dough to make a 10- inch circle or 8 x 10-inch rectangle. Bake for 5-7 minutes or until the dough begins to bubble up and brown. Remove from oven and spread Peach Bacon Jam over the entire dough, leaving ½ inch for crust around the edges. Spread the shredded pork evenly across the pizza, then top with onions and sharp cheddar cheese. Return to oven and bake for 10-12 minutes until the cheese is bubbly.

Peach Bacon Jam

1 pound bacon, cut into ½-inch pieces
1 sweet onion, chopped
4 ripe peaches, peeled and diced
1 cup dark brown sugar

2 tablespoons whole grain Dijon mustard
2 tablespoons Worcestershire sauce
¼ cup apple cider vinegar
2 tablespoons bourbon

In a large cast iron pot, cook bacon over medium high heat until crisp, about 10 minutes. Remove from heat and drain cooked bacon on paper towels. Remove all but 2 tablespoons of bacon grease from the pot and discard the rest. Return pot to stove, add onions, and cook over medium heat, stirring occasionally until softened, about 8-10 minutes. Return bacon to the pot with diced peaches, brown sugar, Dijon mustard, Worcestershire sauce, apple cider vinegar, and bourbon. Bring to a boil, reduce heat, and simmer, stirring occasionally, until jam is thick and glossy, about 30-35 minutes. Remove from heat and cool to room temperature. Serve jam at room temperature.

LJ note: This fancier jam is next on the Donohue family's list—think Keely's dad would get mad if she used his "good" bourbon?

STUFFED MEATLOAF

1 pound ground beef

2 eggs

1 cup Italian bread crumbs

1 teaspoon garlic powder

1 teaspoon salt

1 teaspoon pepper

¼ cup diced pepperoni

¼ cup diced ham

¼ cup shredded provolone

¼ cup shredded mozzarella

1 (15 ounce) can tomato sauce

1 teaspoon dried basil

1 teaspoon minced garlic

¼ cup diced sweet onion

Preheat oven to 350 degrees. In a large bowl, combine ground beef, eggs, bread crumbs, garlic powder, salt, and pepper. In a separate large bowl, combine the pepperoni, ham, provolone, and mozzarella. Place ½ of the ground beef mixture in a meatloaf pan. Top with pepperoni mixture, then top with remaining ground beef mixture. In a small bowl, combine tomato sauce, basil, garlic, and onion, and spread over the top of the meatloaf. Bake for 1 hour. Allow to rest for 10 minutes before serving.

POTATO CRUSTED QUICHE

3 cups frozen hash browns, thawed

⅓ cup butter, melted

½ cup goat cheese

½ cup shredded white cheddar cheese

¼ cup chopped asparagus

¼ cup sliced mushrooms

¼ cup diced sweet onion

½ cup bacon, cooked and crumbled

½ cup diced ham

1 teaspoon salt

1 teaspoon pepper

3 eggs

½ cup milk

Preheat oven to 425 degrees. Press hash browns between paper towels to remove excess moisture. Press onto the bottom and up the sides of an ungreased 9-inch pie plate. Drizzle with butter. Bake for 25 minutes. Remove from oven and add goat cheese, white cheddar, asparagus, mushrooms, onion, bacon, ham, salt and pepper to the crust. In a small bowl, beat eggs and milk then pour over all ingredients. Reduce heat to 350 degrees and bake for 25-30 minutes. Let stand for 10 minutes before serving.

CRANBERRY CHICKEN AND WILD RICE

6 boneless, skinless chicken breasts

1 can whole cranberry sauce

1 packet onion soup mix

1 bottle Catalina dressing

1 box wild rice, cooked per package directions

Preheat oven to 350 degrees. In a 9 x 13-inch baking dish, place chicken breasts evenly in the dish. In a large bowl, whisk together the cranberry sauce, soup mix and dressing. Pour over the chicken. Bake covered with foil for 30 minutes and uncovered for 20 minutes. Serve over wild rice.

SOUTHWEST SALAD
WITH CHIPOTLE RANCH DRESSING

3 leaves Romaine lettuce, chopped

1 (15 ounce) can black beans, drained

1 (15 ounce) can corn, drained

1 avocado, sliced

1 cup shredded Monterey jack cheese

2 Roma tomatoes, diced

¼ cup red onion

¼ cup fresh cilantro, chopped

Chipotle Ranch Dressing

Place all ingredients in a large bowl and toss together. Drizzle with dressing before serving.

If you are feeling fancy or like being a freelance artist, place the romaine lettuce in a bowl then top with remaining ingredients to your liking....we eat with our eyes, right!?

Chipotle Ranch Dressing

½ cup mayonnaise

½ cup sour cream

1 teaspoon garlic powder

1 teaspoon onion powder

1 teaspoon dried dill

1 teaspoon salt

1 tablespoon lemon juice

½ teaspoon pepper

2 chipotle peppers (in adobo sauce)

In a food processor or blender, combine all ingredients until smooth. Store in a sealed jar in the refrigerator for 24 hours before serving to allow flavors to combine.

BRIE AND BACON CAULIFLOWER MAC & CHEESE

1 large head of cauliflower

1 cup heavy cream

1 round of Brie, rind removed

½ cup shredded white cheddar

1 teaspoon salt

1 teaspoon pepper

6-8 slices of bacon, cooked and crumbled

1 cup panko bread crumbs

1 cup grated Parmesan cheese

1 stick butter, melted

Preheat oven to 350 degrees. Cut the cauliflower into small pieces, including the stems, and steam for 5-6 minutes. In a large saucepan over low heat, pour in the heavy cream, then break apart the Brie and add to the saucepan. Stir to combine, then add in the cheddar cheese, salt and pepper. Stir until all cheese is melted and creamy. Add in drained cauliflower and bacon. Stir until all of the cauliflower is coated evenly. In a small bowl, combine the panko bread crumbs, Parmesan cheese, and melted butter. Pour cauliflower mixture into a greased 9 x 13-inch baking dish and top with the bread crumbs, spreading evenly over the top. Bake for 20-25 minutes until golden and bubbly.

CONFETTI COFFEE MUG CAKE

4 tablespoons flour

3 tablespoons sugar

½ teaspoon baking powder

3 tablespoons milk

1 tablespoon oil

1 teaspoon vanilla extract

1 tablespoon of your favorite sprinkles

In a microwave safe coffee mug, mix together all ingredients until smooth. Place in the microwave and cook for 1 minute and 30 seconds. Allow to cool in the microwave for 1 minute. Top with your favorite icing and more sprinkles...because, YES!

Here are two more variations for the kids to try:

For Cookies and Cream Mug Cake, simply *add 2 crushed Oreos into your mixture.* FUN!

For Strawberries and Cream Mug Cake, simply *add 2 diced strawberries into your mixture.* AMAZINGNESS!!!

CHAPTER 5

RECIPE FOR TROUBLE

"Can you show me a fresh design? Something I *haven't* seen a hundred times?" the blonde coed asked as she rapidly flipped through the pages in the massive sample book.

India McKay, tattooist and owner of India's Ink, curled her hand into a fist below the counter, out of view. "Hang out with a lot of my former clients, do you?"

"What do you mean?"

"Basically you just claimed these designs are *so yesterday.* Even when there are several hundred of my designs in that book. Most of which I've never inked on anyone, so it's unfair to act as if you've seen them all before, because that is an impossibility."

Vapid stare from the blonde bimbo. Then her eyes took on a mean glint. "What if I don't like *any* of your *several hundred designs*?"

At that point, India could've salvaged the situation, claiming she'd be happy to revise color and size options of existing images or quote the minimum price for a custom drawing...but Indy had already suffered through a shitastic day. Consequently, she wasn't taking shit from anybody, especially not a customer guaranteed to be impossible to please.

Cut your losses and save your sanity.

Indy pointed to the front of the store. "If you don't like them then there's the door."

Miss Precious wasn't expecting that. "That is so rude."

"So is coming into *my* studio and insulting *my* work." Indy leaned across the counter and practically bared her teeth. "Good luck finding another tattoo artist. You're done here."

An outraged gasp. "You're seriously turning me away?"

"Yep." India did a Vanna White worthy hand gesture at the sign on the wall behind her that stated:

**WE RESERVE THE RIGHT TO REFUSE SERVICE
TO ANYONE—YES, THAT MEANS YOU**

"Me? What did I do besides ask a simple question?"

Then with sarcasm India said, "Omigod, Brittney, you were like...*so* condescending to me. But there's a bright side: at least you'll have a *killer* story to share with your sorority sisters about the time you got kicked out of a tattoo parlor."

"My name is Bella, not Brittney, *asshole*."

"Whatever. Bye-bye."

Little Miss Huffy Pants stormed out.

A heavy sigh drifted across the room. "Obviously, you missed a key chapter in Carnegie's book, *How To Win Friends and Influence People*," India's sister Skylar mused.

"That chick can fuck the fuck off." India slammed the design book shut and walked over to her sister's side of the shared storefront. Half the space housed India's Ink. The other half housed retail products from Sky Blue, the all-natural skincare business Skylar owned. "What are you doing here?"

"Nice to see you too, sis." Sky studied her.

"I doubt that's true, given my mood. Weren't you test batching at the factory today?"

Sky frowned at her. "No. We did that last week. Remember? We talked about it?"

"Vaguely." India sighed and ran her hand through her short hair. "Life has been a blur since school ended."

A look crossed her sister's face—a look of concern that annoyed India.

"Don't start. I'm fine."

"Sure you are. You're snapping at customers, forgetting conversations, ignoring texts and skipping McKay family get-togethers."

"I had a stomachache on Sunday." Indy's gaze narrowed on Sky. "Who told you?"

"No one. I was there. And the fact you didn't know that Kade, the girls and I were there just tells me that something is going on with you."

"Yeah. I was sick."

"It's more than that. I've seen this before—"

"Oh for fuck's sake, Skylar, I'm *not* holed up in my house drinking and doing drugs! I'm still sober, still clean, still going to meetings and I still get pissed off—"

"Any time I ask a simple question about your behavior," Sky snapped back. "Which is normal for you. So can the crap and tell me what's really going on."

I can't because you wouldn't understand.

India stared at her beautiful, perfect, successful sister. Most days she was proud that Skylar had built a thriving business from the ground up. Today, however...it felt as if Sky's success only highlighted the downturn India's business had taken.

When India remained mum, Sky tossed out guesses. "Is everything all right with you and Colt?"

"Yes, we're fine."

"Are the kids acting out again?"

She shrugged. "They're kids. Most days they're fine."

"Is Colt having family issues and you're maintaining a low profile to keep the peace?"

"His relationship with his family is fine. The ranch is fine."

"If every goddamned thing is *fine, fine, fine,* India, then why the hell do you look like you're about two seconds from having a breakdown?"

They glared at one another and that was India's tipping point. She and Sky hadn't fought like this for years. Yes, she understood her sister was only trying to help her. But what Skylar couldn't see—and wouldn't accept—was that she couldn't help this time.

India exhaled. "You know what? I'm calling it a day. I'll talk to you later." She strode through the backroom and grabbed her leather jacket and helmet from the hooks by the door. Once she'd geared up, she climbed on her motorcycle.

Colt was taking care of their children and cooking supper tonight. Since he wouldn't expect her home for a few hours, she could use the time alone to organize her thoughts and figure out a solution for getting out of this funk.

Colt McKay spurred his horse, attempting to cut off the heifer and her calf before they got tangled up in the scrub oaks that divided the draw. It'd been a few years since he'd worked this section of the ranch and he didn't remember if a barbed wire fence still blocked access where the tree line ended. Letting loose a loud "H'yaw" scared the runaway pair and they rejoined the herd. Then he reined his horse around until he was riding even with his cousin Kade.

"Damn, Colt, it's almost like you're a real cowboy, the way you're directing that horse," Kade teased.

"Piss off. I ride plenty. I just prefer using ATVs."

"Just funning with ya, cuz. That stubborn horse usually only responds to Kane."

"You *did* see this fucker try and buck me off earlier, right?" Colt said dryly.

"Yeah. Sorry about that. I appreciate you comin' over and helpin' me move the herd while Kane is gone."

"No problem. You'd do the same." Their business, McKay Ranches was several individual ranches which combined created one massive ranch. Each McKay family ran their own sections. But when manpower ran short, someone in the family helped out. Colt ended up working with his twin cousins Kane and Kade more frequently since his wife, India, and Kade's wife, Skylar, were sisters.

"Kane and fam are supposed to be back next weekend," Kade said.

"Remind me again where they went on vacation?"

"Calgary. Then on to Banff and Lake Louise."

"Beautiful country, I hear. Damn long drive, though."

"Yep."

They rode in silence for quite a while. Neither felt the need to talk just to hear their voices break up the silence. That attitude was the norm for ranchers. Or maybe just the norm for the McKay family.

After a bit, Kade said, "Did Skylar call you?"

"You mean have she and Indy talked? I reckon so, they talk nearly every day. Why?"

"No, I mean did Sky specifically call you and ask to talk to you?"

Surprised, Colt turned and squinted at him. "No. Why would she to that?"

Kade raised a gloved hand and scratched his chin. "I hate bein' in the middle of this. But she's worried about India."

Colt's stomach dropped.

"Sky said she planned to get in touch with you, but apparently she didn't, so now I feel like an ass bringing it up."

"When did Skylar mention this to you?"

Kade scratched his chin again. "Night before last."

"Huh. That's weird. Indy hasn't been actin' differently that I've seen." His mind backtracked to the nights in question. They'd had their normal rowdy supper with their three kids. One evening they'd played a couple of family board games and the next night they'd watched a movie before tucking their little beasties in bed. Then they'd gone to bed themselves for some adult fun. Indy had been a bit more...subdued voicing her pleasure during their sexy time, but he'd chalked it up to her trying not to wake the kids.

"Jesus. Sorry, Colt. Forget I said anything."

"I'm glad you did." He shifted in his saddle. "Did Sky say *why* she was worried about my wife?"

"No. And you oughta know that I'd tell you if had a damn clue about what was goin' on."

"I know you would." When Colt had hit rock bottom years ago with his drinking, drugging, whoring and fighting, Kade was the one who'd gotten him into rehab. That's how Colt and Indy had met; she'd been his AA sponsor.

"Do you want me to ask Sky about it tonight?" Kade said.

"Nah. I'll figure out if something is goin' on." And he'd get the information directly from the source.

"Good enough. We're almost to the next gate anyway, so I'll ride ahead."

An hour later Colt and Kade parted ways and Colt headed home.

When he pulled up to his house, he saw the minivan parked in the driveway, which meant Indy had picked the kids up from summer day camp. Noting the time on the dashboard clock, he hopped out of his truck and climbed into his ATV since he still needed to check his cattle.

After he finished with final chores, he cut through the garage into the mudroom to clean up. As he wiped his hands, he meandered into the kitchen. Scanning the area, he noticed India hadn't started supper. Nothing new. His wife had many talents, but cooking wasn't one of them. That'd never bothered him; between the two of them they managed to keep their family fed. However, he'd sworn she'd promised to make her "famous" Wyoming Pot Roast tonight and he'd been looking forward to it.

Cartoonish music echoed from the living room where his sons Hudson and Ellison played video games. They barely acknowledged him. He gave it a pass... this time.

But his sweet McKenna hopped down from coloring at the dining room table and skipped over to him.

"Daddy!" She hugged his knees and lifted her arms to be picked up. "I missed you."

"Same here, girlie." Hoisting her onto his hip, he smooched her soft cheek.

Her sweet giggle and affectionate nature cracked his heart wide open. He loved his sons fiercely, but this little girl of his was something special. Appearance-wise she'd hit the genetic lottery, a perfect mix of him and India—curly coal black hair, vivid blue eyes, sharp jawline and angular facial features. Even strangers commented on her striking looks. Colt couldn't fathom the attention she'd garner as she matured, so he'd enjoy every moment of her goofy girlhood.

"Did you have a good day at camp?"

She shrugged and fiddled with the buttons on his shirt.

"Where's your mama?"

McKenna didn't answer. In fact, she wouldn't meet his eyes.

A bad feeling whomped him in the gut. Before he pressed McKenna for answers, Hudson said, "She went into her room after McKenna made her cry."

"I didn't mean to," she said so softly he barely heard it.

Cry? Jesus. India usually spit fire if she got upset. He couldn't remember her ever taking to her bed. Especially not in the afternoon, leaving the kids somewhat unattended. His gaze swept over their living space. Toys, clothes and kids' crap covered everything. Maybe she'd had enough of the constant carnage.

He set McKenna down between her brothers and stood in front of the TV. "Boys. You're done. Gimme the controllers."

Wisely, neither son argued.

Colt gestured to the three of them. "Start pickin' this mess up. No one eats until I can see the damn carpeting."

When Ellison, their brainiac argumentative one, opened his mouth to object, Colt sent him a look, thus ending his protest.

Hudson, the oldest, had inherited Colt's tendency to use charm to get his way. He offered a toothy grin and said, "Don't worry, Dad. I got this. Go see if Mom's okay."

Then Colt headed to their bedroom.

The door wasn't locked. The sliver of light from the bathroom skylight allowed him to see a small lump beneath the covers. In two strides, he sat on the bed next to her. "Indy? Are you sick?"

She shook her head.

Reaching over, he smoothed her hair back, his stomach clenching at the cool dampness of her face. "Sugar, are you mad about something?"

Another shake of her head.

"What's wrong?"

No movement of her head, nor did she open her eyes.

"Baby, I can't help you if you don't talk to me. Please. You're scaring me."

India finally looked at him. Her eyes were red-rimmed, her face was puffy, and her lips trembled. "Go take care of the kids, Colt. I need some time alone."

Fuck that.

Not that he'd phrase his reaction that way. He moved to kiss her forehead before he stood. "Don't go anywhere. I'll be right back."

The first thing he did was make a call to his cousin Chassie Glanzer, who lived with her family on a ranch up the road from them. "Hey Chass, I'm in a bind. Can you take the kids tonight and I'll pick them up in the morning?"

"Sure, bring them by," she said without hesitation. "Anything serious goin' on?"

"Honestly, I'm not sure."

"Whatever you need, Colt, we're here."

"I know. Thank you."

Miracle of miracles, the kids were picking up like he'd asked. He said, "Change of plans. You three are goin' for an overnight at the Glanzers'. Quietly grab your toothbrushes, pajamas and backpacks."

Ten minutes later the kids were settled with their cousins.

Ten minutes after that, Colt was back home.

India was still in bed.

Colt stripped down to his boxer briefs and crawled in beside her. Even before he could wrap her in his arms, she curled herself around him, her face finding the spot against his chest where she belonged.

"Cry, scream, talk...whatever you need, Indy. I gotchu." He kissed the top of her head. "It's just us, baby." Another kiss on her crown and he tightened his hold on her.

She cried harder.

The tears dampening his chest burned like acid, but he held her, soothed her without words as he hoped she'd open up to him.

His soul breathed a sigh of relief when she finally started to talk.

"Being with you like this...is the one place I don't feel like I'm failing." She ruffled her fingers through the dark hair covering Colt's broad chest.

"While I appreciate that I'm your safe space, I feel like I've failed you because I don't know what's goin' on." He paused. "Although, I sort of got warning today that things might be coming to a head."

"How?"

"Kade. He said that Skylar was worried about you." Colt's fingers trailed up and down her arm. "Did something happen?"

"Not with Sky, but we did have a fight the day before yesterday."

"Then tell me what happened today that has you hidin' in the dark."

God. How would he react to what'd sent her boo-hooing in her bed? "It'll sound stupid but if you laugh at me, Colt McKay, I swear I will punch you in the dick."

"So noted."

"I had one tattoo appointment scheduled. But she didn't show up. People change their mind often enough that it doesn't usually bother me."

"Why was it different this time?"

"I could claim it's because I've had a crap week. Or I could blame it on burning jealousy that Sky Blue is always so much busier than my studio. Both answers are accurate. But the truth is, after the kids and I got home, the boys played video games and McKenna asked me to color with her. When she finished her page, she asked to see mine. I showed her the doodles I'd done in my sketchbook and she said, 'No mama, I wanna see your new drawing.' When I told her it *was* new, she sighed and said that I *'always, always, always* draw the same thing and it's *always, always, always* boring.' That stung. It's embarrassing to admit I started arguing with a three-year-old."

"That's an easy trap to fall into. I find myself doin' it with Ellison more than is wise. Even when Hudson reminds me it's pointless."

This man. His face was beautiful and his body strong—but it was the size of his heart and depth of his devotion that made her entire being sing with gratitude. He continually reminded her they always had each other's backs, which made it easy to maintain a united front for their kids. "Then McKenna flipped pages in my sketchbook and proved herself right." She swallowed the lump in her throat. "That hit me right where it hurts because I threw a potential client out of my studio this week for accusing me of that very thing. So I'm sitting at the dining room table, wilting under McKenna's disapproval, and I realized my discontent isn't from jealousy over Sky's business, but from being in a creative rut that's affected my business."

Colt gently stoked her back and murmured, "Can you explain that?"

"I'll try." She paused. "There's little variety in the tattoos I'm asked to do. Is it because I work in a rural area and the most popular artwork is also the most clichéd? I mean, how many times can I make a rose look different? Or a butterfly? Or hearts, or skulls, or scrolls, or memorial lettering? I cannot remember the last time I did any ink that challenged me. So I stopped trying." She blinked away more tears. "I've become *that* tattooist, Colt. Bitter about the rebel I used to be who swore she'd never settle for mediocrity."

Colt said, "Okay," in the drawn-out manner that indicated he hadn't reached an opinion. "Keep talkin', sweetheart."

"Skylar tried to get me to talk to her, but she doesn't understand. Her livelihood isn't entwined with her creativity. In fact, it's better for her to rely on what's tried and true. What sells." India's tears fell as she spoke. "I've been taking it out on her the past few months and that's not fair when I'm really mad at myself. I've stagnated. She's flourished."

"Darlin', no disrespect to your sister, and I'm not downplaying her accomplishments, but you're comparing apples and tractors."

She snorted. Her husband had such a unique way of saying things.

"Two things come to mind, so bear with me."

"Okay."

"Bein' a tattooist used to be your vocation, and no offense; it's become more of a hobby. You work when it suits you. Ain't nothin' wrong with that. Nothin' wrong with deciding you've had a good run with your studio and it's time to move on." Colt tipped her chin up to look in her eyes. "I'm not advocating for that."

"What are you advocating for?"

"You. Always only you." He rested his lips on her forehead for a moment. "Close the place down if you want. Hire ten more artists and expand if you want. Just don't doubt your talent."

"I can't help it. The more I think about it the more paralyzing it becomes."

"If you never inked another tattoo again, would you miss it?"

India thought about that. Giving up her space to her sister. Selling her equipment. Being in the house all day every day. Her stomach cramped imagining that scenario.

But it also made her queasy to think of tattooing nothing but hearts, flowers, skulls and scrolls for the foreseeable future.

"Baby, you don't have to decide tonight."

"I know."

"The other point I need to make is..." He sighed. "That one can wait." Colt lowered his mouth to hers, giving her the sweetness she so rarely needed. She preferred his fire, his greed, his sexual intensity since she was the only person who witnessed that complicated side of him.

After a bit, she sighed and snuggled deeper into him. "You know me better than anyone, Colt, and I love you for that."

"But?"

"But this isn't something you can fix for me."

"I wish I could."

"Me too."

Colt didn't suggest she get out of bed and stop wallowing. Her sexy husband didn't try to distract her with sex. He was just there for her in the way she needed him to be.

The next morning, Colt told her that he'd deal with getting the kids to camp if she'd meet him at Dewey's, the family style restaurant in Sundance, for a late breakfast. Since Dewey's was on the same block as their Sky Blue/India's Ink storefront, she didn't think too much of it because they met for meals there regularly.

In fact, she wasn't suspicious when the hostess seated her in the back room. Nor did she give into skepticism when Colt still hadn't arrived fifteen minutes after their meeting time; the man was perpetually late. Not even when the waitress suggested she go ahead and order cued her warning bells.

However, as she shoveled in the last of her omelet and noticed her brother-in-law Carter striding into view, she finally realized she wasn't meeting her sneaky-assed husband at all.

Smiling, Carter slid into the booth seat across from her. "Mornin', Indy."

"Carter." She shoved her plate aside. "Colt sent you."

"Yep."

"I'm gonna strangle him." Mortified, she closed her eyes, afraid she'd burst into tears because Colt had broken her confidence and blabbed her secret fears to Carter, the very definition of a successful artist—the exact opposite of her.

"Don't be mad at him. My brother is gutted because he can't help you." A pause. "And he reached out to me because he thought maybe I could fill that void."

"How much did he tell you?"

"You afraid he broke some promise or trust between you by reaching out to me? I assure you, he didn't. And woman, you know Colton McKay ain't never like that, especially not when it comes to you."

The roiling in her stomach settled. "I guess I'm just paranoid."

"Eh. Comes with the artistic neurosis."

"So, seriously." Instead of meeting Carter's gaze, she watched her fingers folding the corner of the placemat. "What did Colt say to you?"

"Just that you're struggling creatively." She sensed him looking at her. "India, all artists have been where you are...in that doubting zone. Some thrive best in misery and it fuels their creativity. People like us, we need a kick in the ass once in a while. Artist-to-artist, that's what I'm here to do for you."

Her gaze flew to his. "Carter McKay. You're a *real* artist. With commissions and an agent. You're part of a network of creatives...and I tattoo people. What you do and what I do? Not even fucking close to the same thing and you damn well know it."

"Wrong." He rested his arms on the table and studied her. "You make your living from your artistic talents. Same as me. Do you think all the artists in my network create the same type of western art that I do?"

"If I say yes...you'll tell me...?"

"No. But that doesn't mean we don't have similar issues when it comes to the fears, hang-ups and neuroses all artists suffer from."

"You really have the same—"

"Thought process that starts with the 'I suck, that's the ugliest thing I've ever done, I'm a hack, I'm never picking up a pencil again and my career is over' mantra playin' over and over in my head as I look at the piece of shit someone paid me money for? Yep. I usually have a pretty bad case of that at least once a year."

"What do you do?"

"Ignore it. If it lingers, then I try something outside of my current project to find a spark. If none of that helps...I call a friend."

"That's just it, Carter. I don't have any friends in the business anymore. When I first moved to Wyoming from Denver, I kept in touch with my tattooist buddies who lived all over the country. I didn't think it'd be hard to maintain friendships. Then I got super involved in AA here because they needed volunteers, Colt and I fell in love, and we started a family and my focus changed."

Carter lifted an eyebrow. "Regrets about that?"

"None."

"Good. What's preventing you from reaching out to them now? Explaining that you regret losing touch with them. The worst they can say is they're busy or not interested in rekindling the friendship or professional relationship. Or maybe you'll discover they're happy you took the first step and you'll find you have more in common now than you ever did."

India felt a tickle of hope. Maybe she could reconnect with former friends and colleagues. Wouldn't it be great to have that again? To swap ideas and stories. Share problems and solutions.

"See? I can tell that interests you."

"Why didn't I think of this on my own?"

"Life happens." He shrugged. "Once you're mired in that mindset of worst-case scenarios, or what my chef wife calls a recipe for trouble, it's hard to pull yourself out of it on your own."

Indy snorted. "Recipe for trouble. Boy howdy, does that fit. All recipes give me trouble."

"You know what I mean, smarty." His smile faded. "It's easy to turn into an island, and oddly enough, it's really easy to do that living in Wyoming. What I hope you take away from this convo is you aren't alone...unless you choose to be. There are always classes or seminars or webinars that'll keep you up to date on trends and new techniques. Creation might be instinctive, but creative *consistency* requires dedication to a lifelong process of learning. Doesn't matter if you're welding metal, wielding a tattoo needle or whipping up a soufflé."

"How'd you get so wise, Carter McKay?"

"I wouldn't say wise...maybe experienced in all levels of artistic failure and success." Another shrug. "I'd like it if we stayed in touch not just because we're family. The truth is...not a lot of people in our family 'get' what we do."

"So at some point you'll expect an ass-kicking from me, Carter?"

"Absolutely."

She reached out and squeezed Carter's hand. "Thank you for talking to me. Thank you for making the four-hour-round-trip drive here for an hour-long conversation. Thank you for always being a great brother to my husband."

Carter's expression stayed serious. "I owe you, Indy, for saving Colt. I know you'll tell me he straightened himself out. But you'll never convince me he isn't a better man because of you. You believed in him and that allowed him to believe in himself. With you he's grabbed onto the kind of life he wanted but didn't believe he deserved. There's nothin' that I wouldn't do for you."

And she started crying again.

They talked for a little bit longer. India could've bounced things off Carter all day, but she realized she needed to share her revelations with Colt first. He deserved it.

Carter stood. "Now gimme a hug and go get started on them ideas I see churning behind your eyes."

Colt hadn't heard from India all day.

Carter hadn't called him either, so he had no idea how the meeting had gone.

So when he pulled up into the driveway and saw his feisty wife standing next to the ATV, arms crossed over her chest and her stance battle ready, he figured he'd better prepare for a fight.

But as soon as he exited his truck, he had to literally brace himself because Indy launched herself at him. Her arms tight around his neck, her legs wrapped around his waist, holding onto him for dear life.

"Colton McKay, I oughta kick your ass for blabbing to your brother about my whiny-ass-bitch problems. But I just..." She buried her face in his neck. "Love you so much. How do you always know exactly what I need?"

"I don't. But I'm stubborn enough to do whatever it takes to figure it out."

She brushed her lips across his skin and the days' tension left him in a rush, turning him damn near giddy. "Thank you for getting me. Thank you for finding a way to help me."

"Just returning the favor." As always, her praise made him uncomfortable, so he deflected. "So your meeting with Carter was a success?"

"It was like a dark cloud lifted. I went back to the studio, locked the door and spent all afternoon making new plans to get my mojo back."

Still keeping his hands clamped on her tight little ass, he leaned back to gaze into her eyes. "It's always been there, Indy, you just needed help reclaiming it."

Those beautiful eyes narrowed. "Last night you said two things came to mind about my situation and said one would keep. What was it?"

Colt cocked his head. "You tell me, because I'm pretty sure my bright wife figured it out when that dark cloud lifted."

Shadows flitted across her face. "Will she think I'm ungrateful?"

"No, baby. Skylar's been worried about you. On some level she had to know that you two—"

"Can't continue sharing a storefront," she said softly. "I know how successful Sky Blue is only because I'm there running the cash register and stocking shelves. That leaves little time to devote to my business."

"Exactly." Colt nuzzled her cheek. "Like I said last night. You have to do what's right for you. I'll back your play, be your tattoo guinea pig, corral the kids—whatever my talented wife needs to get back on track."

Her contented sigh tickled his ear. "Have I mentioned how much I adore you?"

"A man can't ever hear that too much."

"I freakin' love you, cowboy." She smooched him on the mouth like ten times. "Come on, let's go."

Colt set her on her feet. "If you can hold that thought...I need to—"

"Check cattle. I know. That's why I'm out here waiting for you. Let's get on with it."

He blinked at her. "Sugar, lemme get this straight. You're volunteering to check cattle with me?"

"Yep."

"But you hate doin' cattle checks."

"Ha! For your information, I don't hate checking cattle with you. I can't check cattle with you because we have three kids, and someone needs to stay with them and make sure they don't burn the damn house down."

"Ain't that the truth. But speakin' of kids..."

"They're having an overnight with your folks. As much as I love them, I want us to have a serious talk about my future business plans without interruptions. And I packed us a picnic. Been a long time since the two of us watched the sunset at our favorite spot."

"A picnic?"

"Oh, wipe that skeptical look off your face. I can totally make picnic stuff."

Colt smirked. "Peanut butter and jelly sandwiches?"

She rolled her eyes. "*Puh-lease.* It's a little fancier than that."

Like her "fancy" spaghetti. Or her "fancy" Rice Krispies treats.

God. He loved this woman. He'd be happy eating pine needles as long as she was by his side. "By all means, let's get a move on."

Supreme Lasagna

Wyoming Pot Roast

Pizza Taquitos

Lobster Roll Ups

India's Asian Chicken Salad
with Sesame Ginger Dressing

S'mores Rice Krispies Squares

RECIPES

LJ note: When Suzanne and I were discussing this book, I insisted on having recipes for "noncooks" like India McKay. While Suzanne didn't go with my original suggestion of a "recipe" for spaghetti and a jar of sauce as one of India's specialties, she did come up with these options that are as easy as they are delicious!

SUPREME LASAGNA

2 cups ricotta cheese

2 tablespoons basil pesto

1 (24 ounce) jar of your favorite marinara, divided

1 box "no boil" lasagna noodles

2 cups "leftover" meat sauce marinara*

1 package pepperoni

4-5 button mushrooms, thinly sliced

1 green bell pepper, diced

1 small sweet onion, diced

2 cups grated mozzarella cheese

Preheat oven to 350 degrees. In a small bowl, mix together the ricotta and basil pesto until smooth. In a 9 x 13-inch baking dish, pour ½ cup of marinara and spread to cover the bottom of the dish. Place a single layer of noodles onto the sauce. Next, spread the leftover meat marinara onto the noodles. Place another single layer of noodles on top of the meat marinara. Pour 1 cup of marinara onto the noodles, then spread the vegetables and place a single layer of pepperoni on top. Place another layer of noodles, then spread ricotta mixture on top, and top with mozzarella cheese. Finish with a single layer of pepperoni. Bake for 50 minutes. Allow to rest for 10 minutes before slicing.

*"Leftover" meat sauce marinara is THE BEST THING EVER! The flavors have married together, and you don't have to brown the one pound of ground beef and drain the grease that have been mixed in with your favorite marinara sauce. It is just ready to go!! The leftovers come from spaghetti night. It's as common as Taco Tuesday, right? Place the leftovers in a resealable bag and refrigerate for 2-3 days, if you plan to have the lasagna that soon. If you are waiting longer, simply place the bag in the freezer for later use. When you are ready to make the lasagna, place the frozen bag in a large pot of boiling water. Boil for about 5-10 minutes or until the marinara is completely thawed. -SJ

WYOMING POT ROAST

1 3-4 pound chuck roast

1 packet Ranch seasoning

1 packet Au Jus gravy

1 stick butter

1 (8 ounce) jar pepperoncini, with juice

2 teaspoons dried sage

Place chuck roast in a crockpot. Pour in the remaining ingredients and combine/rub on roast. Cook on low for 8 hours.

PIZZA TAQUITOS

8 flour tortillas
1 (15 ounce) jar pizza sauce
1 cup chopped pepperoni
2 cups shredded mozzarella cheese
1 stick butter, melted
1 teaspoon garlic powder
¼ cup chopped fresh parsley

Preheat oven to 400 degrees. Lay out a flour tortilla and spread a thin layer of pizza sauce evenly over the surface. Place a row of pepperoni down the middle of the tortilla then cover with mozzarella cheese. Roll the tortilla and place seam side down in a 9 x 13-inch greased baking dish. Repeat with remaining tortillas. In a small bowl, stir together the butter, garlic powder and parsley, then brush over the top of the rolls. Bake for 12-15 minutes or until the top of the tortillas are light brown. Serve with remaining pizza sauce.

SJ note: If you want to get a little crazy, add your own favorite toppings. Go supreme, meat lovers, Hawaiian or cheese lovers!!! You can't mess these up. They are simply DELISH!!

LOBSTER ROLL UPS

6 lobster tails, cooked and cut into 1-inch pieces

½ cup chopped celery

⅓ cup mayonnaise

Juice of 1 lemon

¼ cup chopped parsley

¼ teaspoon seasoned salt (I use Lawry's)

6 hot dog buns

4 tablespoons melted butter

In a large bowl, combine the lobster, celery, mayonnaise, lemon juice, parsley, and seasoning salt. Open the hot dog buns and lay flat. Using a rolling pin, roll the buns flat and brush evenly with melted butter. Place about ½ cup of the lobster filling on one end of the bun. Roll up and secure with 3 toothpicks evenly across the roll. Cut in between each toothpick to make 3 rolls. Continue with remaining buns.

Who knew a hot dog bun could be so fancy? -SJ

INDIA'S ASIAN CHICKEN SALAD
WITH SESAME GINGER DRESSING

1 bag of Romaine lettuce

1 box of frozen chicken nuggets (cook as directed on the box)

1 can mandarin oranges

1 (12 ounce) bag chow mein noodles

Combine all ingredients in a large bowl and serve with Sesame Ginger Dressing.

Sesame Ginger Dressing

2 tablespoons soy sauce

½ cup oil

3 tablespoons rice wine vinegar

1 tablespoon sesame oil

1 tablespoon lime juice

1 teaspoon minced garlic

3 tablespoons honey

1 tablespoon ground ginger

Combine all ingredients in a jar and shake, shake, shake!! Refrigerate for at least 4 hours before using. Shake before each use.

S'MORES RICE KRISPIES SQUARES

1 stick butter

1 package mini marshmallows

7 cups Rice Krispies cereal

1 cup Teddy Grahams, roughly chopped

1 cup milk chocolate chips

In a medium saucepan over low heat, combine butter and marshmallows. Stir until all marshmallows are melted. In a large bowl, add Rice Krispies and Teddy Grahams. Pour the marshmallow mixture over the mix and stir to combine. Add in the chocolate chips and stir, then pour into a greased 9 x 13-inch baking dish. Spray your hand with nonstick spray and pat down the treats until evenly distributed in the dish. Allow to cool before slicing.

CHAPTER 6

UNBREAK MY DISHES

It happened exactly as his wife had predicted.

He watched in horror as the serving platter, heirloom dessert plate, glass pitcher, and serving bowl slipped from his hands and shattered on the kitchen tile around his feet. Her warning—*Boone West, stop tempting fate by carrying that many dishes at one time*—reverberated in his head as the ultimate *I told you so.*

Sierra was going to fucking kill him.

His first thought? To flee. He'd book a flight to Antarctica—it'd be warmer there than the cold shoulder she'd give him *for the rest of his life.*

Yet, knowing her, she'd track him down and figure out a way to sic a flock of Emperor penguins on him to peck out his eyeballs while she watched.

Calm down and think, man.

He could...buy replacements. Since this tableware was only used when they entertained...if he could track down exact replicas before next Sunday's football games, she'd never have to find out about his little slipup or that her beloved dishes were cleverly placed clones.

Lying to her...that's really the option you're going with?

It's not lying. It's finding a way to prevent a marital rift.

Besides, he'd really like to keep his balls attached to his body.

What about the family heirloom? Where you gonna find a plate like that? Especially when you know that's the one she cares the most about?

The front door slammed and for a brief moment, Boone saw his life flash before his eyes.

But it wasn't Sierra strolling into the kitchen, just his best buddy Raj. "Hey, B you ready to..."

Raj took one look at the broken crockery on the floor and froze. Then his wide-eyed gaze met Boone's. "Been nice knowin' you, man...but I gotta bail."

"Wait. You just got here! Where are you going?"

"Back home to pick out a nice suit for your funeral."

"Hilarious." Boone threaded his fingers together and rested them on top of his head as he eyeballed the mess. "Although there ain't nothin' funny about this."

"No, there ain't since you brought this on yourself." Raj sighed. "Boone. Buddy. Me'n Lucinda Grace lived here for over a year, which means we *both* heard Sierra drilling the *smaller stacks, fewer cracks* warning into your dumb ass all the damn time."

"I know, I know. I'm an idiot, all right? I was in a hurry and I lost my balance and I only managed to catch the cheap glass vase."

"Didja get cut anywhere?" Raj asked hopefully, "because bleeding might be the only thing to save you."

"Not a damn scratch on me."

"Shame."

He eyed the mess with guilt and sadness. "Will you please help me clean this up?"

"Yeah. I'll get a broom."

Boone had lined up the biggest chunks and was snapping pictures of them when the garbage can thunked next to him.

"What in the hell are you doin'?"

"Making sure I have enough images of each piece so when I try and—"

"Please tell me you're not gonna try and glue these back together? They're pulverized beyond recognition."

"Jesus, no, I'm not that dumb. I'm taking pictures because the only option I have is to buy identical replacements and hope Sierra never notices."

A pause lingered. "So that's your play? You're gonna lie to her?"

Boone sent Raj a sharp look. "I'm fixing the mess the best way I know how. And you have to promise me not to tell Lu about this, Raj. I'm serious." Lu and Sierra had been roommates and BFFs when Boone and Sierra had reconnected. It just happened that Raj and Lu fell in love at first sight. "Promise me."

"No can do, man. You might not have a problem lying to your wife, but I have a big one lying to mine."

His buddy might rethink that after he and Lu had been married for longer than three weeks, but Boone didn't relay that bit of marital wisdom.

"However, I promise not to specifically share this incident, but if she asks me point blank about it, I ain't covering your ass just to get my own handed to me."

Boone grabbed the broom and swept up the shards. Then he vacuumed the area, dumped the evidence into a black garbage bag and stowed it in Raj's jeep.

"Good thing you haven't gotten around to installing those security cameras yet," Raj said with a shit-eating grin.

"Fuck off. I am riding the knife's edge about this FUBAR."

"I can tell." Raj clapped him on the shoulder. "Let's hit the gym like we planned. That'll help."

"Are you crazy? I have to go shopping right now."

Raj shook his head. "You are messed up if you think you can just waltz into Target and buy replacements. Especially a replica of her family heirloom, which is an antique."

"Fine. What do you suggest?"

"You've gotta do recon first. Online. So grab your laptop and we'll figure out your options while you're buying me lunch."

Taking pictures of the identifying marks on the bottom of each broken piece had saved Boone's bacon.

Luckily, the turquoise and blue serving platter was in stock at Williams Sonoma. The frosted glass margarita pitcher, part of a glassware line at Pier One, was still available. The fancy bowl...that proved trickier to track down, as it'd been a limited-edition piece of patterned Fiestaware sold only in the southwest. Thankfully, he'd located one in a boutique store in downtown Scottsdale and he hadn't balked at the asking price.

That left the dessert plate. The ugly dessert plate. The ugly antique dessert plate that was a family heirloom—a fact Sierra reminded him every single time he handwashed it. The gaudy floral plate rimmed in gold wasn't her style at all. It definitely didn't belong at their Arizona-style tailgating parties, alongside tinfoil containers of chicken wings, hearty appetizers on skewers and bowls of chip dip. Still, she pulled it out of the china cabinet every Sunday during football season and piled it high with the dessert of the day. Since the McKay-kateers always commented on the plate, Boone assumed it'd been a bequest from someone in the McKay family.

Boone swigged his beer and brought up the eBay website. "Raj, look at that last bunch of photos and spell out the name on the bottom of that antique plate."

Without hesitation, Raj called out, "L-i-m-o-g-e-s," and Boone carefully typed it into the search engine.

"Are you fucking kidding me?"

"What?"

"Seventy-eight thousand results popped up. How in the hell am I ever gonna narrow it down? It there an edition number or something by the stamp?"

"Might've been, but there's no way to know for sure since this pic is just of a shard." Raj adjusted the screen so they could both squint at it. "Maybe if you narrow the search down to...color or pattern?"

Boone snorted. "Is extremely ugly an option?"

"Only for your face if you can't find a replacement."

"Piss off. How about you narrow down the search to gold-rimmed on your phone and I'll go with floral and we'll see if anything matches.

A solid thirty minutes passed before Boone saw the plate. "Ha. Fucking *finally*. Got it."

Raj leaned over. Looked from the close up of the floral image on Boone's phone to the close up of the plate on the computer screen. "Appears to be a match to me. Does it give dimensions?"

"Yep. It has the same square-ish deep-set center and scalloped fluted edges in cobalt and gold. This has to be it."

"How much is it?"

Boone squinted at the symbols. Wasn't his dyslexia causing issues; the price was listed in euros. "Need a currency calculator. Six hundred sixty-one euros is...?"

Raj punched it into his phone. "Jesus. Seven hundred and eighty US dollars."

"That is a lot of money for that ugly thing." He scrolled over the shipping info. "Oh. It gets better. Plus a hundred bucks to ship to the US from France." He dry-scrubbed his face. "Fuck. Okay. It is what it is. If I purchase now, they can guarantee delivery by Thursday."

"Boone. Stop. Think about this. You gotta fess up, man. Save yourself nine hundred bills and four more days of stress. You have no guarantee that it'll get here in one piece anyway."

"There's buyers' insurance, which is another forty-five bucks. And I don't have a choice, Raj."

"Whatever. It's your money. But you know it's gonna be worse when she finds out what you've done."

"*If* she finds out," Boone corrected.

"Oh, you sneaky motherfucker, did you really think I wouldn't *notice*?" Sierra McKay West demanded, as she stared into her china cabinet on Tuesday evening.

She might not have even realized the antique dessert plate wasn't in its usual spot, if she hadn't jabbed the bottom of her foot on something, which led to her rolling the kitchen rug back and finding two chips of pottery. Blue and gold chips that were no doubt from the gilded edges of the Limoges plate.

So she'd intended to see if the plate had gotten chipped...only to find the entire piece gone.

Boone had sneakily shifted a couple of vases and bowls around to try and mask the empty spot, but all his attempts had done was draw her attention to what *wasn't* there. She allowed her mind to backtrack to Sunday afternoon and the other three pieces of dishware she'd used for the party.

Snagging the margarita pitcher by the handle, she examined the opening. Smooth as a baby's ass. Which meant this wasn't her pitcher. One night, her senior year in college, she'd gotten aggressive stirring the tequila concoction with a glass rod. Glass on glass had nicked the inner rim. Sierra intended to pitch the pitcher, but Lu had convinced her that flaws only made things—and people—more interesting, so she'd kept it. You'd never notice the chip if you didn't know exactly where to look. Apparently, Boone hadn't seen it and had replaced the pitcher, believing she wouldn't know the difference.

Wrong.

Next, she examined the big serving platter. It looked the same. So either he hadn't broken this one or he'd succeeded in locating the perfect replacement.

Lastly, she picked up the fancy bowl they used for tortilla chips. It was a funky piece of Fiestaware they'd received as a wedding gift. Sierra ran her hands along the inside and outside. When her fingers brushed the bottom, tackiness from a price sticker caught her thumb.

Busted.

Maybe you should've washed it after you took it out of the box, bonehead.

Sierra closed the china cabinet door and wandered into the living room, pacing as she weighed the pros and cons of her next move.

Confronting him immediately would be the mature thing to do. Demand to know why he thought he could buy his way out of trouble after destroying her serving ware, especially when she'd repeatedly warned him to stop his reckless dish endangerment by carrying too many pieces at once.

Boone hasn't done the mature thing, so why should you? He should've confessed instead of literally sweeping it under the rug and lying about it.

But she couldn't accuse him of lying because he hadn't lied about anything... yet.

Which led her to wonder what scheme he'd conceived to explain the demise of the Limoges plate. Had he saved the pieces? Would he do a *whoops* on Sunday, scattering the fragments across the tile as if he'd *just* dropped it?

She'd almost like to see if he could pull that off.

Chances were higher that a panicked Boone had probably logged onto eBay. Or maybe that china match site where one could buy individual replacement pieces for thousands of dishware sets, in an attempt to avoid confrontation— aka confession.

Even if he had found a duplicate, he'd likely paid through the nose for it, since hand-painted Limoges pieces from the late 1890s weren't cheap or easy to come by.

Funnily enough, Sierra owned a second plate, identical to the first one.

Oh, Boone baby, it's gonna be so much fun fucking with you—just to see how long it takes you to crack.

Sierra was in their bedroom, cooling down from her forty-five-minute stretch on the elliptical machine, when her hunkyalicious hubby burst into the room, wearing only a tight T-shirt and boxer briefs. Even before he said hello, he made a beeline toward her. His lips landed on her mouth, his hands clamped onto her ass, and he carried her into their master bathroom. He managed to remove his right hand from her butt cheek long enough to turn on the water in the shower.

Then he trailed his lips up her jaw and breathed heavily in her ear. "Hi, baby. Shower with me."

As if she could refuse that. Coherent thoughts sailed right out of her head when faced with Boone's bossiness and that banging body.

It turned into a race; who could get naked first. She toed off her shoes while pulling her sports bra over her head. Her athletic shorts and underwear hit the floor the same time as his.

Boone guided her into the oversized shower, pressing her back against the marble so he could watch her nipples tighten at the sudden cold. And his mouth was right there, tongue flickering across the tips before he sucked them hard.

"Boone."

"Touch me," he panted against the upper swell of her breast. "I've been waiting all damn day to feel your hands on me."

The passion in this man was staggering at times. All that male need directed at her and she gloried in it. "Step under the water."

He poured shampoo into his hand and slapped it on the top of his head. His army career kept his dark hair in a short military cut, so the soap and suds portion wouldn't last long.

Sierra flattened her palms and ran them over the thick slabs of his pectorals, stopping to dig her fingers into the mat of chest hair that gave him an extra punch of manliness. She scraped her nails down the divots that separated the ridges of his six-pack abs—marveling at how dedicated her soldier was to maintaining strength and health.

And stamina. So much stamina. *Whoo-ee.* Lucky her.

She swept her thumb over his belly button, not lingering because it was one of his ticklish spots. But also because the edge of her wrist bumped the head of his cock and she needed to get her mitts on that bad boy immediately.

He groaned when she fisted her hand around the wide shaft, arching into the stream of water when she started to stroke.

Then Boone's soapy hands were on her shoulders and inching down the center of her body as he latched onto her neck with his hungry mouth. Gifting her with sucking kisses and running his tongue over the pulse pounding in her throat. "I love you," he whispered. "I love that we can have this whenever we want."

This meaning time together. She'd spent the majority of the first year of their marriage traveling for her job, so now Boone happily made up for time they'd lost at every opportunity.

Sierra's strokes on his dick stuttered for a moment when Boone's hands slipped around to squeeze her ass.

His lips found their way back to hers when her mouth opened on a gasp. His kisses sent her into a dreamy state where her entire world existed in his touch, the slick slide of the hard planes of his body against her softer curves, the steam surrounding them, the steady pound of her blood in her heart, her lips, her ears and between her legs as her body readied for the possession of his.

Sierra released another groan when Boone gently spun her to face the wall.

"Tell me how you want it," he murmured against the nape of her neck. "I'll give it to you any way you like."

She turned her head to catch the drops of water dripping from his chin, her tongue rubbing against the bristles of his five o'clock shadow. "Slow," she murmured back.

"Slow it is." He curled his hand on the inside of her knee and lifted her leg, setting her foot on the bench beside them. Then his palms skated up the outside of her body and he pressed her hands against the wall. "Stay just like that."

Once she'd braced herself, Boone took himself in hand, lowered his pelvis and drove into her. He immediately cupped his right hand over her mound, so he could feel his cock moving in and out of her as he worked her clit.

Oh yes. She'd needed this.

And he was a master at multitasking, rubbing and teasing her pussy as he kissed her. Soft lips skimming her shoulders. Teeth on the back of her neck. A tilt of her head, allowing him to inflame her with openmouthed soul kisses.

He kept up the slow rhythm until faster strokes became a necessity. Thrusting harder, increasing the friction on her clit until the moment she broke, arching into him, rocking her hips as she came in rippling waves.

Boone's climax started as hers ended and the quicker, harder pace created the perfect storm and she came again.

In a state of mind-scrambled bliss, Sierra moved beneath the shower spray so she could finish her shower, his body shoring up hers as she shampooed, rinsed and conditioned.

The sweet man even dried her off, tucking the towel beneath her breasts before he wrapped his towel low on his hips. He smooched her mouth. "Want a beer?"

"No. I'll take a sparkling water, though."

Later, as they were lying in bed, Sierra on her laptop and Boone on his phone, she offhandedly said, "I found this killer recipe to try. It's been ages since we've hosted a poker game, so I thought we'd invite Raj and Lu over tomorrow night. Super informal, just appetizers, booze and a simple dessert while we destroy them at Texas Hold 'Em."

He immediately froze.

Poor baby. Are you panicked at the idea of me prowling in the kitchen and discovering your duplicity?

Man, it was so freakin' hard to pretend to be absorbed in the article on her screen.

"That's...social of you to want to cook after work since you save that time-consuming task for weekends."

"Eh. I have to go to the store anyway. What do you think?"

"Have you talked to Lu this week?"

Sierra said, "Nope. But she's always up for fun on Hump Day."

Boone snorted. "Her and Raj will be humping as soon as he's off duty, so I doubt they'd get redressed and come over even for your delicious appetizers."

"True. Well, it was a thought anyway."

He leaned over and kissed her shoulder. "A sweet thought. And you can always save the recipe reveal for Sunday's football party."

Oh, you'd like that.

That meant the replacement piece would be here before Sunday. But not by tomorrow.

He probably thought he was in the clear as far as thwarting her party idea.

Lucky thing they had family around that were always up for an impromptu food and game night.

Let the games continue.

Boone parked in the garage and dragged ass out of his SUV. It'd been a rough day at the VA, but he preferred dealing with patients to getting buried in tons of paperwork. Since his position as an active duty RN was an experiment between the army and the VA, he never knew what was in store for him on a day-to-day basis and he had to be adaptable.

After removing his boots and uniform in the laundry room, a mouth-watering aroma greeted him when he walked into the kitchen. He didn't see his wife anywhere until he noticed the massive refrigerator door was open.

Sierra shut the door with a swing of her hip and faced him with a smile.

His wife was a freakin' knockout. Especially dressed in her corporate-America-meets-50s-pinup styled clothing. Usually she changed immediately when she got home, but today, she still wore her red stilettos with the polka-dot bows on the toes and she'd slipped on an apron to protect her dress. "Hey, baby."

"Hey yourself. Something smells good."

"It's those appetizers I was telling you about."

He kissed her cheek since her lips were thickly coated with red lipstick. "You're makin' them just for me?"

"Sorry to burst your bubble but there're not just for you. My dad and Rielle are in town so I invited them over." She unrolled a log of cookie dough from its plastic wrapper. "I knew you wouldn't mind."

"Are they here now? Christ. I'm in my damn skivvies."

Sierra rolled her eyes. "They're not here yet. But you'd better shower because they'll be here any minute. I have just enough time to get this dough sliced and on the cookie sheet for baking."

That statement stopped him in his tracks. Wait. She was baking cookies? That meant...

Fuck. She'd notice the goddamned antique plate was missing.

He had zero good options.

Except get your ass back here and help out and maybe—just maybe—you can avoid a massive fucking fight in front of her dad, who already thinks you're ham-handed, by distracting her with other dishware.

Might've been the fastest shower he'd ever taken.

Sierra raised an eyebrow at him. "You are excited for those appetizers if you're already done getting cleaned up."

"What do you need help with? Want me to set the table?"

"It'd be a big help if you'd get down the crystal lowball glasses and the bottle of Crown apple." She smirked at him. "I know you think I'm bossy, but don't stack them. It's an easy way to chip the edges or drop them."

Normally he'd retort that he wasn't an idiot, but he'd disproved that on Monday. "I'm on it."

When he returned to the kitchen, Sierra was on her phone. "No, Dad. It's not a big deal. We can do this another night. Stay there and take care of Rielle." Pause. "Send her our love and tell her we hope she feels better soon. Love you too." She hung up and swiped her brow with the back of the oven mitt she wore. "Well, that sucks."

"What's going on?"

"Rielle is sick and they're not coming over. So it's just us for dinner."

Boone rubbed his hands together. "More appetizers for me."

She laughed. "You might as well pour us each a drink while I'm getting the serving trays, since there's a lot of food." She started toward the china cabinet but the timer on the oven went off and she whirled back around.

Saved by the bell.

"I'll get the serving platters." As soon as he stood in front of the cabinets, he realized something was very, very wrong.

The ugly antique plate was in its usual place.

What the ever-loving fuck?

He closed his eyes. Reopened them.

And the family heirloom was still there, like his own personal Tell-Tale Heart.

Or maybe the plate was possessed, like the sinister cymbal-playing monkey that just kept showing up even after being tossed away.

Boone felt a chill trickle down his spine.

"Problem?" Sierra whispered directly in his ear and Boone barely stopped himself from shrieking like a teenaged scream-queen.

"Ah...no. Just wondering which one to use."

"Use the bigger turquoise one. I know how much you hate handwashing the Limoges piece and it is your night to do dishes."

The Fried Mac and Cheese Bites were delicious, and he was glad he didn't have to share.

He cleaned up the kitchen while Sierra showered and made some calls. Every so often his gaze would stray to the china cabinet.

Seemed like that goddamned plate was mocking him.

When he put the turquoise serving platter back, the ghost plate tilted forward, brushing the back of his hand and he nearly screamed again.

Enough. He needed reinforcements. He fired off a quick text to Raj:

BW: Tell me I'm not goin' crazy.

Raj: S'up?

BW: U saw the pieces from my accident on Monday, right?

Raj: Yeah. Y?

BW: It's back. The broken plate.

Raj: The one u ordered?

BW: No. It gets here tomorrow. I checked the tracking. It hasn't been delivered yet.

Raj: WTF? Then where'd that one come from?

BW: IDK. I'm freaked out.

Raj: *makes the sign of the cross* Same. That's some Stephen King shit right there.

BW: I don't even wanna walk by the cabinet.

Raj: Afraid the dishes will come to life and start singin' "Be Our Guest"?

BW: FU. If I'm somehow killed by a mysterious slash to my carotid, you gotta tell S the truth about the killer platter and save her.

Raj: I gotchu 👊

Boone watched TV. Before he went to bed, he took one last trip into the kitchen to look at the ugly antique plate to make sure it was still there.

"Everything okay?" Sierra asked as she shuffled toward the refrigerator in her pajamas.

"Fine. Grab me a water too, please."

She said, "Catch," and started to throw it.

"No!" He leapt in front of the plastic projectile, it bounced off his chest and landed on the floor.

"Boone. What the hell is wrong with you?"

"Nothin'. But honey, you've got lousy aim, and I ah…envisioned the water bottle hitting the china cabinet and breaking shit."

She rolled her eyes. "Whatever. I'm more worried about you breaking shit."

Distract her from that broken train of thought.

Making a growling noise, he hoisted her into a fireman's hold and ran to their bedroom, her laughter ringing in his ears, all thoughts of possessed plates fading from his mind.

After Sierra left for work the next morning, Boone hauled himself out of bed and readied himself to head to the gym since he had the day off. As much as he hated to give into his paranoia, he distrustfully eyed the plate as he filled his water bottle and chowed down a protein bar.

Boone's "honey-do" list was short. He cleaned off the pool patio with the leaf blower. Then he tested the pool's pH levels, checked the sprinkler system, and fixed the latch for the side gate.

Covered in dirt and sweat, he took a long shower. With the towel wrapped around his waist, he stepped into the bedroom and froze.

The possessed plate was perched on the bed.

He was losing his damn mind.

Grabbing the plate, he threw open the bedroom door, yelled "Sierra!" and stalked down the hallway into the kitchen.

"You don't have to yell; I'm right here. What do you need?"

"An explanation for this."

His sexy-ass wife leaned against the counter, holding a container of yogurt in her hand and wearing a puzzled look. "Why on earth are you running around half-naked with that serving platter?"

Boone carefully set the plate on the counter. "You know, don't you?"

"Know what?"

He took a deep breath and blurted out, "That I broke two of your serving pieces—including your family heirloom plate—and a pitcher and a bowl. I swear my life flashed before my eyes as each piece hit the floor. So I panicked and decided it'd be better to replace the pieces instead of coming clean." He pointed to the Limoges plate. "But I have no idea where that came from. The one I ordered from France is supposed to be here today, so that's not it. And I'm a little freaked out that it's some kind of magical, self-repairing platter of evil."

She started laughing. "A magical, self-repairing platter of evil? Dude. You're playing too much Skyrim."

"Then how else can you explain it?"

"Logically." Sierra gave him that superior you're-in-for-it-now smile. "I have more than one plate and I've been fucking with you."

His jaw dropped.

Sierra jabbed the air with her spoon. "And before you get that indignant male look, I'll point out that I've yet to hear *any* apologies. Yes, there are a few things you need to ask my forgiveness for, and no, I'm not telling you what they are."

Boone blushed—such a rarity for him that she almost let him off the hook.

Almost.

"I am sorry I ignored your warnings about stacking dishes. If I'd listened to you, I might've only broken one thing when I tripped over the rug, instead of four."

"And?"

"And I'm so sorry that I tried to hide what I'd done. A totally wrong way to handle it and I promise to tell you about any dumb and embarrassing shit I do that affects you, even if it makes me look like an idiot." He scrubbed his hands over his face. "Even if I had gotten away with it, I probably couldn't have kept it a secret for very long because it feels wrong to hide anything from you. I know that now." Boone glanced over at her. "Babe, I feel really bad that I broke your family heirloom."

Sierra turned and set aside her yogurt. "Yeah, about that. Umm...since we're in full disclosure mode. When I said that plate was a family heirloom, I didn't mean it was an heirloom from *my* family."

"What? Explain that."

"It's actually a pretty funny story." She rested her backside against the counter and crossed her arms over her chest. "The same weekend we began gutting this house to renovate it, my next-door neighbor was having a garage sale. So I wandered over there, introduced myself and started browsing. Lots of kids' stuff and sports equipment—nothing that interested me. Then I happened upon a stack of dishes. I picked up one piece, flipped it over and saw the Limoges stamp. It surprised me to see each piece with a two-dollar sticker on it."

"Two dollars?" Boone repeated.

"Yeah. And since I'm not the type who wants to screw over the seller because she wasn't aware of the value of what she had, I asked her if she knew how much Limoges dishware sold for."

"What'd she say?"

"She and her husband were getting divorced. They'd gotten the dishes from her nasty mother-in-law as a wedding gift and anytime she came over for a meal, she'd demanded her daughter-in-law use that 'heirloom' dishware. The neighbor had to listen to her mother-in-law brag about how much they were worth. So to spite both of them, she was selling the pieces for nothing, and if she didn't sell them, she planned on taking them to the gun range and blowing them to smithereens."

Boone's eyebrows rose. "That's some vindictive shit."

"Uh-huh. So I bought the two identical plates and a serving bowl for six bucks. And just for fun, I took them to an antique appraiser who's friends with my dad. You know, thinking I'd found a couple of gems I could resell. He told me the dishes were fakes."

"What?"

"Yep. They weren't much worth more than I'd paid for them. But because I was just setting up my own house and didn't have many dishes, I kept them and used them."

"Wait. What happened to the matching bowl?"

"I barely nicked the edge of the bowl on the sink and the whole thing shattered. No big deal, right? Since I'd only paid two bucks for it." She nudged him. "That's why I told you to be careful with the plate. I knew firsthand how easily it'd break."

A confused look darted through his eyes. "But your McKay cousins always talk about that fancy plate like you were lucky to get a family heirloom."

"No, my cousins teased me relentlessly about how hideous the plate was and how happy they were to see the ugly pattern covered up with good food. They assumed the plate had to have sentimental value from the other side of my family if I insisted on using it every week. Turned into a family joke." She shrugged. "I've never been in love with the plate, but it has a helluva history behind it." That's when she noticed Boone had gone a little pale. "What's wrong?"

He groaned. "Jesus. I'm an idiot. If I would've told you the truth...I wouldn't have spent almost a thousand bucks to hide my crime."

Sierra stared at him in disbelief. "You..."

"Bought an authentic Limoges plate from a vetted antiques dealer in France and paid a rush charge to have it shipped here? Yep."

"Boone."

"I brought this on myself." He gestured to the cabinet. "The others were only slightly easier to replace, but they weren't cheap either. And Christ, I sound like my damn uncles, but it was an expensive lesson for me to learn."

The doorbell rang.

Managing a tight smile, he said, "That'd be your replacement plate. Which I have to sign for."

Now Sierra felt guilty. A thousand bucks wasn't chump change to her hard-working soldier.

He returned with a package and set it on the island counter between them. "I'm so sorry, baby. I can guarantee it won't happen again."

She moved into his arms and they held each other in silence for a long time.

Then he pulled away. "Stay here. I'll be right back." He cut through the laundry room into the garage. A minute or so later he reappeared holding a long, flat cardboard box. "For you."

After slicing through the tape, she peeled back the packing material and discovered an oversized serving platter that matched the Fiestaware bowl. She looked up at him. "Boone. Honey. This is gorgeous."

"It was at the store where I bought the replacement bowl. I figured you'd want it, but I'm not sure what the protocol is for gifts. Lots of guys say to never give your wife household items for Christmas or birthdays, so I'd planned to hold onto it until the right time."

Protocol. Spoken like a true military man. "It is the perfect time. I love it. Thank you." Sierra twined her arms around his neck and kissed him. "I love you. This can be our family heirloom piece. It has a good story behind it too."

Boone kissed her. "I'll be careful with it, I promise."

And she believed him.

Bourbon Butter Tarts

Buffalo Shrimp Tacos
with Blue Cheese Dressing

Fried Mac & Cheese Bites

Cheesy Buttermilk Bites
with Smoked Jalapeno Jelly

Prickly Pear Margarita

Sierra's Brownies

RECIPES

BOURBON BUTTER TARTS

1 refrigerated pie crust

1 ½ cups dark brown sugar

½ cup softened butter

1 teaspoon vanilla extract

2 tablespoons bourbon

2 eggs

Preheat oven to 375 degrees. Line a muffin tin with 12 cupcake wrappers. Roll out the pie crust and cut out 12 circles using a 3-inch cookie/biscuit cutter.* Press each one down into the cupcake wrapper and press along the sides. In a large bowl, combine remaining ingredients and pour into each tin until the filling meets the top of the pie crust. Bake for 15 minutes. Allow to cool for 10 minutes before serving.

If you do not have a cookie/biscuit cutter, not to worry! You can cut out 12 3-inch squares and they will taste just as sublime as the tarts made with circles. -SJ

BUFFALO SHRIMP TACOS
WITH BLUE CHEESE DRESSING

3-4 cups flour

1 tablespoon salt

1 tablespoon pepper

3-4 cups panko bread crumbs

3 eggs

1 bag of 21-30 count shrimp, peeled, deveined and tails off*

1 bottle of buffalo sauce

8 flour tortillas

Oil for frying

1 bag shredded iceberg lettuce

Blue Cheese Dressing

Heat oil to 350 degrees in a Dutch oven or deep fryer. Place the flour in a large bowl and sprinkle with salt and pepper. Place the bread crumbs in a large bowl and sprinkle with salt and pepper. In another large bowl, whisk the eggs together until smooth. Dredge the shrimp in the flour, then egg and lastly the bread crumbs. Fry about 6 shrimp at a time in the oil for 2-3 minutes or until golden brown. Place on paper towels to drain. Repeat with remaining shrimp. Toss the shrimp in the buffalo sauce when ready to serve and place 3-4 in each tortilla. Top with lettuce and Blue Cheese Dressing.

*Not a shrimp fan? Substitute boneless skinless chicken breasts cut into 1-inch pieces. -SJ

Blue Cheese Dressing

6 ounces blue cheese

⅓ cup buttermilk

1 cup sour cream

¼ cup mayonnaise

1 teaspoon Worcestershire sauce

½ teaspoon salt

½ teaspoon onion powder

Combine all ingredients in a resealable jar. Refrigerate for 4 hours before serving.

FRIED MAC & CHEESE BITES

3 cups Bisquick

3 eggs

3 cups panko

Oil for frying

Salt and pepper

Leftover Mac & Cheese

Heat oil to 350 degrees in a Dutch oven or deep fryer. Remove leftover mac and cheese from the refrigerator and cut into 1-inch cubes. In a large bowl, add the flour. Dredge each cube in the flour and place on a parchment lined cookie sheet. Freeze for one hour. Remove from freezer and dredge in the blended eggs and then the panko. Fry in the hot oil for 1 minute or until golden brown. Drain on paper towels.

Mac & Cheese

1 box elbow macaroni

5 tablespoons butter, divided

2 tablespoons flour

1 cup heavy cream

1 cup milk

1 cup shredded sharp cheddar cheese

1 cup shredded mozzarella

1 (8 ounce) block cream cheese

2 teaspoons salt

1 teaspoon pepper

Preheat oven to 350 degrees. Bring 4 cups of salted water to a boil. Add pasta and continue to boil for 8-10 minutes or until the pasta is cooked through. Drain pasta and set aside. In a medium saucepan over low heat, melt 3 tablespoons butter and gradually

whisk in the flour until a roux forms. Add the heavy cream and milk, whisking constantly until thickened. Then, stir in the cheddar cheese, mozzarella, and cream cheese. After you have a smooth cheese sauce, stir in the pasta. Pour pasta into a 9 x 13-inch baking dish. Bake for 20 minutes and serve.

LJ note: Okay, these are so freakin' good I can't even begin to tell you! This is another Beach Babes recipe I laid claim to as soon as I popped one of these in my mouth.

CHEESY BUTTERMILK BITES
WITH SMOKED JALAPEÑO JELLY

½ cup melted butter, divided

2 cups self-rising cornmeal

2 cups buttermilk

1 egg

¾ cup sharp cheddar cheese

¾ cup Monterey jack cheese

Preheat oven to 450 degrees. Place ¼ cup butter in a 9 x 13-inch baking dish. Place in the oven for 5 minutes to allow the dish to get hot. In a large bowl, mix together the remaining ingredients and pour into hot baking dish. Bake for 20 minutes. Allow to cool then cut into 1-inch squares. Serve with Smoked Jalapeño Jelly.

Smoked Jalapeño Jelly

12 smoked jalapeños

1 cup apple cider vinegar

5 cups sugar

1 pouch liquid pectin

12 (4 ounce) jelly jars or 6 (8 ounce) jelly jars

In a smoker on 350 degrees, place 12 jalapeños directly on the rack. Smoke for 2 hours. Remove skin and stem and place in a food processor. Add in 1 cup apple cider vinegar and puree for 1 minute. In a large saucepan mix the jalapeños and sugar together and bring to a roaring boil. Allow to boil for 10 minutes. While the mixture is still boiling, add the liquid pectin and stir continuously for 1 minute. Then ladle the mixture into your jars, leaving ½-inch headspace. Apply caps and let jelly stand in refrigerator until set, about 12 hours, or transfer to your pressure cooker to seal for a longer shelf life. If you are not using a pressure cooker to seal the jars, the jam must stay refrigerated. Refrigerated jams are good for about 3 months. Sealed jars have a shelf life of about 18 months to two years.

LJ note: I'm pretty sure Sierra would've helped Keely make jam if she'd been in Wyoming - ha

PRICKLY PEAR MARGARITA

2 ounces tequila (I use Patron Silver)

2 ounces sweet and sour mix

1 ounce triple sec

1 ounce lime juice

1 ounce prickly pear syrup

Fill a shaker with ice. Pour tequila and remaining ingredients in the shaker. SHAKE!!! Serve in a margarita glass. Salt on the rim is optional.

SIERRA'S BROWNIES

Salted caramel brownies baked on top of chocolate chip cookie bars and finished with marshmallows, coconut, M&Ms, mini peanut butter cups and raspberry buttercream frosting.

1 roll chocolate chip cookie dough

1 box brownie mix

9 unwrapped soft caramels

¼ cup mini marshmallows

¼ cup shredded coconut

¼ cup M&M's

1 teaspoon coarse sea salt

1 batch Raspberry Butter Cream Frosting

Preheat oven to 350 degrees. In a 9 x 9-inch greased baking dish, spread out the cookie dough to completely cover the bottom of the dish. In a medium bowl, mix together the brownie batter per package directions. Pour over cookie dough, then place the caramels evenly on the brownie mix, submerging halfway into the batter. Sprinkle with sea salt. Bake for 30 minutes. Remove from oven and sprinkle with remaining ingredients except frosting. Return to the oven and bake for 5 minutes. Remove from oven and allow to cool completely then spread icing on top and cut into squares.

Raspberry Buttercream Frosting

4 cups powdered sugar

2 sticks butter, softened

1 teaspoon vanilla extract

2-3 tablespoons milk

½ cup raspberries, pureed

In a medium bowl, using a hand mixer, combine all ingredients until smooth.

Cowboy Cocksucker

Jelly Donut

Wyoming Wildfire

Kinky Pink Lips

Toxic Bitch

The Slutty Mermaid

CHAPTER 7

Ⱦames' Gang Drink Recipes

There's usually lots of laughter and booze whenever I get together with readers. While I've been banned from holding James Gang parties in Kim and Meredith's room at future conferences, I know the next time we're together, we'll be adding these new drinks to our list of favorites!

SHOTS *and yes these are meant to be knocked back in one go*

Lorelei's Signature Drink...Cowboy Cocksucker**

½ ounce butterscotch schnapps   ½ ounce Southern Comfort
½ ounce Bailey's Irish Cream

Layer in a shot glass and shoot it back.

**When Lorelei is the bartender it is one SHOT GLASS of each of these boozes

Jelly Donut

1 ounce Chambord   Sugared lime wedge
½ ounce Bailey's Irish Cream

Layer ½ ounce Chambord, Bailey's, ½ ounce Chambord in a shot glass. Shoot it, then suck on the lime wedge. I swear it tastes just like a Jelly Donut!

Wyoming Wildfire

1 ounce Koltiska whiskey or   Dash or ten of Tabasco sauce,
whiskey of your choice   depending on how hot you want it
1 ounce Fireball

Layer in shot glass and finish with Tabasco. Or put the Tabasco in first and layer with booze. Make sure you have a bar napkin handy to wipe your tears.

MIXED DRINKS

Kinky Pink Lips

3 orange slices

4 cherries

1 teaspoon cherry juice

2 ounces Kinky Pink Liqueur

2 ounces peach schnapps

1 ounce pineapple juice

Lemon-lime soda (Sprite or 7UP)

In a cocktail shaker, smash 2 orange slices and 3 cherries with 1 teaspoon of cherry juice. Shake and strain into an 8 ounce glass that's filled half with ice. Then pour in Kinky, schnapps, and pineapple juice. Top with lemon-lime soda and garnish with an orange slice and cherry.

Toxic Bitch

2 ½ ounces vodka

1 ounce tequila

1 ounce blue (or orange) curacao

1 ounce orange juice

Lemon-lime soda

Lemon and lime slices

Rim edge of 8 ounce glass with lime juice and sugar. Add ice into glass, pour in vodka, tequila, curacao and juice before topping the glass with lemon-lime soda. Garnish with lemon and lime slice.

LJ note: Listen to "Cold Hard Bitch" by Jet while imbibing

The Slutty Mermaid

1 ounce tropical vodka
(like Smirnoff Mango Passion Fruit)

1 ounce blue curacao

1 ounce Midori melon liqueur

1 ½ ounce pineapple juice

1 ½ ounces Malibu coconut rum

½ ounce grenadine

Pineapple and lime slices

Mix all ingredients with ice in cocktail shaker. Pour in sugar-rimmed martini glass, garnish with pineapple and lime.

Character References in *Cowboy Bites*

Rough Riders Series

Cord and AJ McKay – *Cowgirl Up and Ride*

Carter and Macie McKay – *Rode Hard*

Colby and Channing McKay – *Long Hard Ride*

Keely West McKay Donohue and Jack Donohue – *All Jacked Up*

Colt and India McKay – *Branded As Trouble*

Sierra McKay West and Boone West – *Unbreak My Heart*

Other Books by Lorelei James

Rough Riders Series (in reading order)

LONG HARD RIDE

RODE HARD

COWGIRL UP AND RIDE

TIED UP, TIED DOWN

ROUGH, RAW AND READY

BRANDED AS TROUBLE

STRONG, SILENT TYPE (novella)

SHOULDA BEEN A COWBOY

ALL JACKED UP

SLOW RIDE (short story)

RAISING KANE

COWGIRLS DON'T CRY

CHASIN' EIGHT

COWBOY CASANOVA

KISSIN' TELL

GONE COUNTRY

SHORT RIDES (anthology)

REDNECK ROMEO

COWBOY TAKE ME AWAY

LONG TIME GONE (novella)

SILVER-TONGUED DEVIL

Rough Riders Legacy Series

UNBREAK MY HEART

Wild West Boys Series
MISTRESS CHRISTMAS (novella)

MISS FIRECRACKER (novella)

Blacktop Cowboys® Series (in reading order)
CORRALLED

SADDLED AND SPURRED

WRANGLED AND TANGLED

ONE NIGHT RODEO

TURN AND BURN

HILLBILLY ROCKSTAR

WRAPPED AND STRAPPED

HANG TOUGH

RACKED AND STACKED

SPUN OUT

1001 Dark Nights - Blacktop Cowboys® Series novellas
ROPED IN

STRIPPED DOWN

STRUNG UP

TRIPPED OUT

WOUND TIGHT

The Mastered Series
BOUND

UNWOUND

SCHOOLED (digital only novella)

UNRAVELED

CAGED

Single Title Novels
RUNNING WITH THE DEVIL

DIRTY DEEDS

Single Title Novellas
LOST IN YOU (short novella)

WICKED GARDEN

BALLROOM BLITZ

Need You Series
WHAT YOU NEED

JUST WHAT I NEEDED

ALL YOU NEED

WHEN I NEED YOU

Want You Series
I WANT YOU BACK

WANT YOU TO WANT ME

Mystery Novels Written as Lori Armstrong

Julie Collins Mystery Series

BLOOD TIES

HALLOWED GROUND

SHALLOW GRAVE

SNOW BLIND

BAITED (novella)

DEAD FLOWERS (novella)

BAITED/DEAD FLOWERS

Mercy Gunderson Mystery Series

NO MERCY

MERCY KILL

MERCILESS

Other Books by Suzanne M. Johnson

Southern Bits & Bites

Southern Kid Bits & Mom Bites

Southern Bits & Bites:
Our 150 Favorite Recipes

Writing with Lexi Blake

Master Bits & Mercenary Bites

Master Bits & Mercenary Bites~Girls Night

Writing with J. Kenner

Bar Bites: A Man of the Month Cookbook

Writing with Kristen Proby

Indulge With Me: A With Me in Seattle Celebration

Writing with Larissa Ione

Dining with Angels: Bits & Bites from the Demonica Universe

Writing with Kristen Ashley

Dream Bites Cookbook: Cooking with the Commandos

INDEX

ABOUT THE AUTHOR: LORELEI JAMES

Lorelei James is a *New York Times, USA Today,* and *Wall Street Journal* bestselling author. Her award-winning books include steamy western romances in the Rough Riders series, the Blacktop Cowboys® series, the Wild West Boys series, contemporary romance in the Mastered series, the Need You series, the Want You series and the Rough Riders Legacy series, as well as several stand-alone novels and novellas. Lorelei is also the alter-ego of *USA Today* and *Wall Street Journal* bestselling mystery author Lori Armstrong (loriarmstrong.com) whose Shamus Award, Willa Cather Literary Award and High Plains Book Award winning works include the Julie Collins mystery series and the Mercy Gunderson mystery series. Lorelei lives in western South Dakota—yes, by choice—with her husband, and Copper, their crazy corgi, who has made their empty nest years more interesting.

CONNECT WITH LORELEI JAMES

Blog loreleijames.com/blog

Facebook facebook.com/LoreleiJamesAuthor

Twitter twitter.com/loreleijames

Website loreleijames.com

Instagram instagram.com/loreleijamesauthor

Facebook Discussion Group facebook.com/groups/loreleijamesstreetteam

Newsletter loreleijames.com/newsletter

Lorelei's Most Frequently Asked Questions loreleijames.com/faq

Receive text messages when Lorelei has a new release
loreleijames.com/text-messages

Follow Lorelei on Bookbub bookbub.com/search?search=lorelei+james

ABOUT THE AUTHOR: SUZANNE M. JOHNSON

Suzanne Johnson is the *USA Today* bestselling author of three cookbooks, and the recipe developer for six other books with: Lexi Blake, J. Kenner, Kristen Proby, Larissa Ione, and Kristen Ashley. A family-trained south Georgia chef, Suzanne has been cooking all her life, creating not only unique food, but precious memories of meals shared with family and friends. In all her books, Suzanne shows that making delicious meals doesn't have to be complicated—they just have to be made with love.

CONNECT WITH SUZANNE M. JOHNSON

Website southernbitsandbites.com

Facebook facebook.com/SouthernBitsAndBites

Instagram southernbitsand_bites

Made in the USA
Middletown, DE
18 March 2021